Custom Guitars

ACOUSTIC
GUITAR
GUIDES

Custom

String Letter Publishing

G u i t a r s

A Complete Guide to Contemporary Handcrafted Guitars

Publisher: *David A. Lusterman*

Editorial Director: *Jeffrey Pepper Rodgers*

Editor: *Simone Solondz*

Assistant Editor: *Teja Gerken*

Design and Production: *Kajun Design*

Cover Design: *Gary Cribb*

Production Director: *Ellen Richman*

Marketing Manager: *Jen Fujimoto*

Front cover photograph: *Jerry Timm headstock, courtesy Jerry Timm.*

Back cover photographs: *Jim Redgate nylon-string, Zeidler engraved tailpiece, back of an Ed Claxton steel-string, National Reso-Phonic tricone, Froggy Bottom heel cap, and Schoenberg Soloist.*

Photographs on cover flaps: *Ted Megas Appollo tailpiece, Mike Baranik instruments, and Kent Everett flattop.*

Photographs on opening pages: *Ric McCurdy carves an archtop; glimpses of guitars by John Monteleone, George Smith, Alister Atkin, and Minstrel Guitars.*

Photograph on back page by Rory Earnshaw.

Printed in China through Palace Press International.

All rights reserved.

This book was produced by String Letter Publishing, Inc.

PO Box 767, San Anselmo, California 94979-0767

(415) 485-6946; www.acousticguitar.com

Library of Congress Cataloging-in-Publication Data

Custom guitars : a complete guide to contemporary handcrafted guitars.

    p. cm. -- (Acoustic guitar guides)

  ISBN 1-890490-29-6

   1. Guitar--Construction. 2. Guitar--Customizing. 3. Guitar makers. I. Series.

ML1015.G9 C87 2000

  787.87'192--dc21   00-030811

Contents

Introduction

Alex de Grassi

I PLAYED A GUITAR for the first time in 1965. It was a nylon-string Aria that my mother had given to my older brother to encourage his interest in singing. A few years later I removed all the frets to see if I could make a fretless guitar, a disastrous experience that led me to put the frets back on and abandon any aspirations I might have had for the art of lutherie. It was significant, however, in that it marked my first experiment in the search for an instrument that better suited my needs as a player. In a primitive and fleeting sense, it was my first custom guitar.

Since then I have owned many guitars. Along the way I discovered that the steel-string guitar had a sound that best expressed the music I wanted to play. Eventually I also discovered that one guitar might not cover all my needs as a player. Even after I bought my first really good guitar, a Martin D-18, I kept my old Harmony with the impossibly high action because it was better for playing bottleneck and slide. Then came the Les Paul, a succession of 12-strings, and a short-lived infatuation with the banjo. In those days, I had neither the interest nor the financial resources to be a collector. I was simply trying to find instruments that felt good and inspired me to play.

The search eventually led to the discovery of independent luthiers and small factories. Not only can these builders afford to be extremely picky about their craftsmanship and the materials they choose, they can also build guitars that incorporate custom specifications for fingerboard width, body depth, neck profile, and any number of other details. Different combinations of tonewoods, tops, and bracing can produce radically different sounding instruments. Color, attack, sustain, balance, ease of playing, and volume are qualities that most players consider, but different musical styles and personal preferences create the demand for instruments tailored to the individual. Fingerstyle players usually look for something different than flatpickers, classical players have different considerations than jazz players, and everyone's hands are unique.

With the ever increasing cross-fertilization of musical styles, many players seek instruments that combine the qualities of one kind of guitar with those of another. As a solo player with an eclectic musical background, I have always looked for a steel-string with the range of color traditionally attributed to classical guitars and a fingerboard width somewhere between a classical and a steel-string. Today, many luthiers are combining the qualities of these and other traditions, not to mention those wilder hybrids that incorporate features of other stringed instruments (both real and imagined).

This book encompasses a wide spectrum of the work of some of today's finest luthiers. Whether you are a collector, a seasoned player, or a novice searching for your first custom instrument, these pages will serve as both a resource and a document of an art form that is constantly evolving in response to the demands and imagination of today's players. The authors are some of the most knowledgeable builders, writers, and guitar aficionados active today. Their insights into the history and art of lutherie will guide you through this gallery of contemporary custom guitars.

The New Golden Age of
Handcrafted Guitars

Rick Turner

In many areas of art and craft, there is a generally held perception of a Golden Age—a time when the endeavor was pure, technical mastery was at its highest, and the results left to posterity are of a never-to-be-matched quality. The Parthenon, the Sistine Chapel, Dutch master portraits, Chippendale furniture, 17th- and 18th-century Cremonese violins, the Renaissance are all accepted as peaks. Now, at the beginning of the 21st century, the state of lutherie is right up front and in the present tense. Don't look back; you are living in the Golden Age of Lutherie.

Up until the 1960s, steel-string guitar making in this country was dominated by factories, when the prevailing names were C.F. Martin, Gibson/Epiphone, Guild, Harmony, and Stella. The instruments of Washburn, National, and the various brands made by the Larson Brothers in the first half of the 20th century represented a kind of "silver age" of production guitar making, and the 19th- and early–20th-century work of luthiers was little known. The best-known early modern luthiers were John D'Angelico and Boston's Strombergs, all specialists in archtops.

In the late '60s and early '70s, things began to change, as pioneer builders like Michael Gurian, Stuart Mossman, Richard Hoover, Bob Taylor, Augustino LoPrinzi, Jean Larrivée, and J.W. Gallagher challenged the notion that steel-string guitars needed to be built in a factory. But these builders had to overcome a lot of opposition and mistrust. Choosing to buy an off-brand guitar was a brave act for a guitarist who might have reservations about resale value and who could easily buy a great, reasonably priced used guitar in the days before the explosion of vintage fever.

But there were weaknesses in the guitars produced by the major factories during the folk guitar boom of the '60s. Guitars tended to be heavier built than those of earlier decades, and quality sometimes suffered as factories doubled and redoubled their output. At the same time, a new generation of self-taught luthiers was learning to repair and restore vintage guitars, and some were starting to build instruments that embodied the qualities of their favorites. These budding builders came to the craft with great passion and inventive spirits, but their most important characteristic was a willingness to share the ideas and techniques that had previously been closely guarded secrets. This openness led to tremendous advances in tooling, materials, and techniques. If there is anything that separates the guitar-building factories of the past from the

Ric McCurdy shapes a neck.

luthiers of the present it is this willingness to open up their shops, notebooks, and minds to one another. At this millennial milestone, there are no secrets in guitar building, and anyone who tries to claim such proprietary knowledge is likely to be laughed out of the business. The real secret is that, at its highest level, guitar making is still a lot of work and requires a great deal of skill.

Of course, along with the advances in the craft have come philosophical debates, mostly centered on the definition of "handmade." The amount of hand work in a guitar does not necessarily differentiate a factory-built guitar from one built by a luthier. There are some amazing hand-made instruments with parts carved by a computer, and even industry giants like Martin, Gibson, and Taylor maintain custom shops that employ incredibly skilled luthiers capable of the highest level of craftsmanship. Somewhere between the luthier who builds a few instruments a year and sells them directly to the guitarist and the factories that make thousands of guitars a year are the limited-production shops that sell wholesale to music stores—Santa Cruz, Collings, Breedlove, Goodall, CFox, and National Reso-Phonic at the bigger end of the scale as well as Gallagher, Huss and Dalton, Tippin, and others. Many of the limited-production shops use high-production–style

James Olson adds frets to a beautifully inlaid neck.

tooling, including the latest CNC (computer numerical control) wood-machining centers. These makers try to combine the efficiency of production tooling with the skill of hand-tuning. Their guitars may have a CNC-carved neck and CNC-inlaid fingerboard as well as an ear-voiced top and hand-carved braces.

At the other end of the scale, solo luthier Jim Olson's main helper is a Fadal CNC machine. Is a one-off Gibson, like the recently completed Super 400 fretless bass built by Phil Jones, more or less handmade than an Olson? Does it matter? It does at the day-to-day level. The real issues facing a small-shop luthier are the blending of all the parts into a cohesive and synergistic whole. This is achieved in the daily choices that are made in selecting one piece of wood to go with another and the individualizing of those parts to make a complete instrument. The typical factory guitar is made to a set of blueprints, and though there may be a wood-grading system to select materials for certain models, one top brace will be cut and shaped exactly like its brothers and sisters for hundreds or thousands of guitars.

The basic design of a factory guitar is likely to be fairly conservative—based on input from a marketing department and focus groups with the goal of pleasing stockholders. The modern handmade guitar is likely to be something quite different. The experienced hand-builder will modify each of the wood parts—thinning here, scalloping there, lightening here, laminating there—to bring all the parts in concert for the desired sound. The best luthiers can achieve amazing consistency—far more than typically exists in the materials themselves—through this tuning and voicing process. A stiffer top will be braced lighter and may even get a heavier bridge, a dreadnought-size instrument will be given a top with a particular cross-grain stiffness, and a floppier top may be used on a parlor-size body.

In design, too, the hand-builder offers more options than most factories. You can get anything from an exact replica of your favorite 1932 vintage piece to the outrageously fanciful and individualistic creations of Fred Carlson, William Eaton, or Harry Fleishman. Where are you going to go if your muse demands an eight-string guitar or if you want to play Hindustani-style slide? What about a fretless nylon-string guitar or a baritone with a 28-inch scale length? You now have your choice of dozens of great guitar makers standing by their phones waiting for your call—that is, if they are not two years back-ordered. With many luthiers, you can discuss and choose every individual stick of wood that goes into your guitar. I recently took an order for a jumbo that will have southeast Asian rosewood back and sides, a German spruce top, Adirondack spruce braces, and a Brazilian mahogany neck laminated with red, white, and blue veneers. The client chose the color scheme and selected every piece of wood.

Modern decorative lutherie is also at a historical zenith. Inlay designs have broken through the traditional constraints of concept and execution, and the quality of much of the inlay work being done today totally eclipses the work of the past. Inlay specialist Larry Robinson literally wrote the book on modern guitar ornamentation, and other luthiers such as Renee Karns and Grit Laskin have advanced the state of the art to incredible heights.

One of the greatest things about buying a guitar directly from a builder is the relationship forged through the process of discussing needs, ideas, and possibilities. Many luthiers have long-term patrons who have bought several instruments just as an art collector might specialize in the paintings of a particular artist. Jeff Traugott has a client who buys one guitar a year, Abe Wechter has built several instruments for John McLaughlin, and Linda Manzer has built multiple instruments for both Pat Metheny and Bruce Cockburn. These are truly creative collaborations in which the luthier becomes an essential part of the music-making process.

The average household in America has few heirloom-quality objects—things that will give pleasure to many generations to come. Commissioning a luthier to build a high-quality acoustic guitar, however, represents a chance to both own something wonderful now and to pass that object on to future generations. Few things combine art and utility in the service of art as beautifully as acoustic guitars.

Steel

-String
Flattops

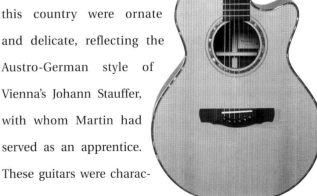

The steel-string acoustic guitar, especially the flattop, has enjoyed a renaissance for the past decade or so. A vital part of that revival has been the steady increase in the number of independent luthiers who constantly push the guitar's design and decoration in new directions. Though some may criticize such stretches beyond tradition, it is helpful to remember that the instrument's development has always depended on variety and innovation from diverse sources. The steel-string guitar is the ultimate melting-pot instrument, a musical kaleidoscope of the diverse cultures and trends that have shaped the music of North America.

Although many immigrant guitar makers landed in New York, the arrival of C.F. Martin in 1833 would change the future of the American guitar. The first guitars he made in this country were ornate and delicate, reflecting the Austro-German style of Vienna's Johann Stauffer, with whom Martin had served as an apprentice. These guitars were charac-

Facing page: **Jeff Traugott eight-string Model R with two extra A strings (high and low) and fanned fretboard.** | Above left: **Kim Walker Style B Special with bearclaw spruce top and rosewood binding.** | Above right: **Kevin Ryan Mission grand concert cutaway with spruce top.**

terized by a figure-8 body shape, with upper and lower bouts of almost equal size, and a long, curving head-stock with the tuners all on one side. Soon these styles gave way to more plain and sturdy designs, probably in response to the more rough-and-tumble lifestyle of many musicians in the New World.

The American guitar that evolved by the mid–19th century was no doubt in-fluenced by guitar makers other than Martin, but un-fortunately little record of these other contributors has survived. The new instru-ments had a more slender body shape whose upper bout was much smaller than the lower, a rectangular bridge, and a symmetrical head-stock with three tuners on each side. Perhaps the most important development was beneath the guitar's top, where Martin began to use an X-bracing pattern that was better able to balance the pull of the strings on the bridge. This bracing design would prove invaluable decades later, when American guitars would be strung with steel strings instead of gut.

The guitar didn't really catch the American public's attention until the late 1800s, and it still lagged far behind the banjo and mandolin in popularity. Guitar and man-dolin duets and ensembles were the rage, and players began to clamor for larger and louder instruments. In the new century, American guitars—regardless of who made them—usually looked a lot like what Martin had been making since Civil War days. Huge factories in Chicago and New York sprang up to meet the rapid-ly increasing demand. Lyon and Healy, the juggernaut of early mail-order purveyors of musical merchandise, sold its Washburn guitars and less-er brands in every price range. Sears catalogs, and others like it, penetrated even the most remote rural areas, bring-ing guitars and instruction books on how to play them everywhere the mail would go.

Celtic-inspired inlays on a custom Martin.

With the distribution of inexpensive guitars came the more widespread use of steel strings, primarily because they were much less expensive and far more durable than gut. When Hawaiian music swept the country in the late teens, steel-string guitars really came of age. The popularity of the new Hawaiian guitar style, played with a metal bar on steel strings high above the fretboard, even prompt-

Left: **Dunwell Ponderosa dreadnought with padauk back and sides and Sitka spruce top.** | Right: **Wechter Pathmaker 12-string acoustic-electric with double cutaway and tree-of-life fingerboard inlay.**

Left: **Don Musser classical-style steel-string with slotted peghead, abalone binding, and torch abalone inlay.** | Top right: **The Valencia grand concert from Guild's custom shop features a 1954 body design and art deco inlay.** | Above right: **Inlaid pickguard on the Mark Angus Carl Verheyen Studio model.**

ed the stodgy Martin company to finally build instruments for steel strings. What had been a slow evolution away from gut strings soon became a frenzy, as 78-rpm records with hot flatpicking by Nick Lucas and other guitarists like Roy Smeck pushed the guitar from its backup role.

In the 1920s, the steel-string flattop guitar finally made it to America's hit parade of popular instruments. Martin offered its first model with steel strings for standard playing style in 1922, and the rest of the company's guitars were offered with steel strings in the next few years. Most of the nation's other guitar companies had long since made the switch. Gibson finally relented and began making flattop guitars as well as archtops in 1926, and by 1928 a quite respectable Gibson flattop endorsed by Nick Lucas was offered with typical Gibson fanfare. The American steel-string guitar quickly became a common sight in the hands of crooners and cowboys. Even the now-legendary Robert Johnson, and most blues singers like him, used the flattop guitar. Musical variety shows such as Chicago's National Barn Dance and Nashville's Grand Ole Opry made stars of singers like Gene Autry who hauled fancy flattop guitars wherever they went. After decades

Above: **A quartet of Mike Baranik guitars, left to right: koa parlor guitar, walnut SJ, rosewood SJ, and maple jumbo.**

of being buried in ensembles and drowned out in bands, the guitar was finally at center stage.

At this point, C.F. Martin Sr. would have hardly recognized the steel-string flattop. The turn-of-the-century mandolin and five-string banjo fads had left American gui-tars with a unique style of pearl inlay and other decoration. The Hawaiian guitar craze had made hardwood tops of koa or mahogany an alternative to spruce. The four-string banjo's influence was seen in longer, narrower necks with more frets clear of the body. The archtop guitar's populari-

Bozo Guitars Bell Western cutaway 12-string.

With steel-string guitars, it's balance that you're after. The steel-string is such a powerful instrument because of the string tension, it's almost like reigning it in instead of letting it fly. With the classical guitar, it's a study in learning how to allow the wood to release the sound.

—**Kent Everett**

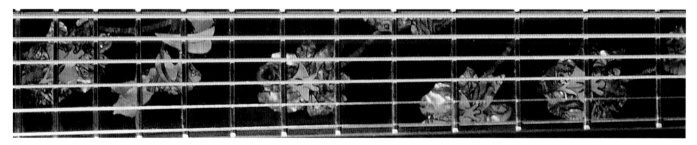

Top right: **Kent Everett Milano series L model with custom orchids inlay.** | Above: **Everett fingerboard with custom orchids inlay in mother-of-pearl and paua abalone.**

ty had prompted most manufacturers to abandon the slotted headstock in favor of a solid one and to offer sunburst finishes. The flattop steel-string was like a magnet that attracted features from other popular fretted instruments, a trend that continues to this day.

The steel-string guitar's body and its tone had undergone an even greater transformation. The constant need for more volume, and especially more bass response, resulted in a stream of larger guitars. Soon the most popular of these oversized instruments were those with a shallow curve at the waist and deep sides, putting the maximum number of cubic inches possible under a player's arm. Martin called these behemoths dreadnoughts, while

Gibson had similar models with more rounded shoulders. First widely offered in the 1930s, these models steadily increased in popularity. Along with bigger guitars came heavier strings and the more widespread use of flatpicks. Purists may have shuddered, but the new American guitar was heard everywhere, from street corner to concert stage, and on every radio wave in between.

Left: **Stunning all-koa Goodall jumbo with island scene inlay.** | Right: **Hank to Hendrix custom Pearl Deluxe small-body with original artwork by Kimber Cavanagh.**

Left: **McPherson 777 with alternative soundhole.** | Right: **Fleishman asymmetric steel-string with double tuned sound ports, morning glory inlays, and fanned frets.**

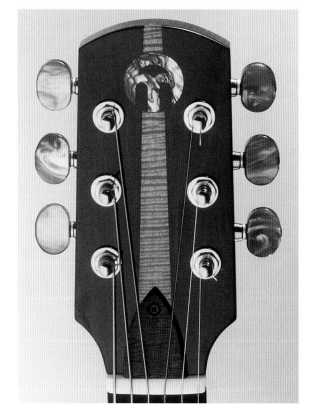

Left: **S.B. MacDonald acoustic jumbo with claro walnut body and cedar soundboard.** | Top right: **The flamed koa back of an Ed Claxton model EM.**

Above right: **The Rio rosewood and koa Mayfield Custom headstock on a Northworthy steel-string.**

It's ironic that the guitar's greatest period of innovation was in the midst of the Depression, and though its popularity increased, many guitar companies didn't survive. By the early 1940s, the field of competitors had narrowed, and the rush to develop new models was over. The next two decades were rather quiet in comparison, with only fine-tuning of existing guitar styles rather than the development of any new ones.

The rising popularity of folk music in the late 1950s and early '60s put heavy demand on companies like Gibson and Martin, who now had new competition from Guild. Except for some half-hearted attempts to market flattops

Left: **Evergreen Mountain New York with cedar top, koa back and sides, 12-fret neck, pierced vine and leaf soundhole rosette, and maple, koa, and ebony binding.**
Center: **H.G. Leach Cremona with highly flamed redwood top and lion inlay.** | Right: **Mauel parlor guitar with flamed black walnut body and redwood top.**

The ultimate thing in building is to have players come to my shop, to sit down and listen to them play, and then absolutely zero in on their taste in every aspect of the instrument, whether it's some far-out new kind of inlay or just the purfling that goes around the top. So it's two people's creativity going into the instrument, not one. You wouldn't believe the stuff we come up with sometimes. Until it's right, I can't stop.

—**Michael Hornick, Shanti Guitars**

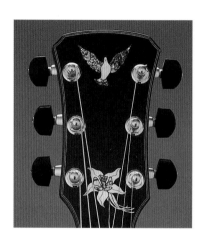

Top: **Silver, ivory, and abalone columbine inlay in a Shanti peghead.** | Above: **Shanti L model cutaway with koa back and sides and German spruce top.**

with magnetic pickups mounted in the face, however, the only real change was the rebirth of 12-string models. This time the guitar's renewed popularity spurred innovation in the form of modern materials, as witnessed by Ovation's success with fiberglass bowl-back guitars introduced in the late 1960s. When it came to how steel-string guitars were played, the biggest change was the renewed popularity of fingerpicking and the decline in popularity of heavy-gauge strings.

The real change in the acoustic guitar market during the late 1960s and early '70s wasn't new models but new makers: the emergence of independent guitar makers and small companies intent on gaining a small share of the growing market. Gurian and Mossman produced significant numbers of guitars, but their rapid growth also proved to be their undoing. At the same time, individuals like Steve Klein pushed acoustic flattop design in new directions. Soon there was also new flexibility in how the steel-string flattop was tuned, as Will Ackerman, Alex de Grassi, and others began to explore an ever-growing list of open tunings, giving solo guitar music a new sound. Since their needs often went beyond what conventional guitars from a factory could deliver, such players were more likely to seek the help of individual luthiers.

Though big guitar companies suffered during the guitar slump of the early to mid-1980s, most independent builders and smaller companies weathered the hard times more easily. Larrivée brought a new awareness of Canadian steel-string styles, while Taylor Guitars, one of the first companies to effectively push slim necks and low string action, became a serious contender as well. Cutaways became more common as the acoustic flattop entered a new era and attracted electric guitarists. As new piezo-based pickup systems improved, the acoustic guitar became much more versatile and could hold its own in any setting. By the end of the 1980s, it was clear

Queguiner jumbo custom with ebony fingerboard and abalone trim.

Ralph Bown L-00 cutaway with cedar top and marquetry trim.

that the acoustic flattop was not just alive and well, but thriving.

In the '90s, acoustic guitars by independent luthiers steadily gained a larger and larger share of the market. Biennial conventions of both the Guild of American Luthiers (GAL) and the Association of Stringed Instrument Artisans (ASIA) provided opportunities to share techniques, and detailed articles in publications by these organizations provided young luthiers with a fast track to producing first-rate guitars with just a few years' experience. Luthiers began to exhibit their guitars publicly, and at some point individual builders simply reached a critical mass that made buyers more confident. For those who like wide-ranging choices, small builders usually offer more options in body styles, woods, tone, and decoration than the big guitar companies. As the photos here demonstrate, the acoustic guitar now reflects a wider range of influences than ever before.

—*Richard Johnston*

Left: **Langejans RGC-6 rosewood and spruce grand concert.** | Right: **Santa Cruz OM with 45-style abalone trim.**

Top left: **Florentine cutaway on a Judy Threet Deluxe D.** | Above left: **Intricate inlay on a Moonstone fingerboard.**

It's well known that individually handcrafted guitars are different from factory guitars, and that the difference has value. In the last ten or 15 years, it has become quite clear that there are small shops building instruments that are equal to or superior to the best production instruments— and these are highly personalized in terms of voicing, ornamentation, and function.

—Michael Millard, Froggy Bottom Guitars

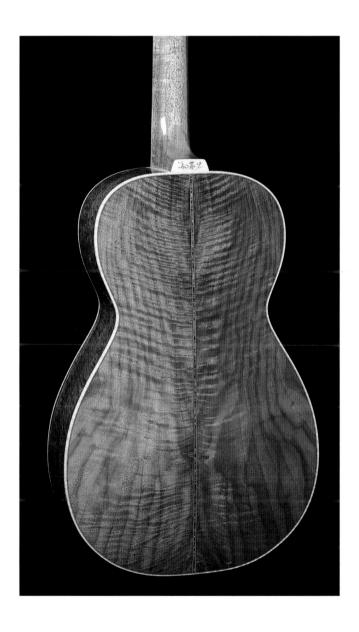

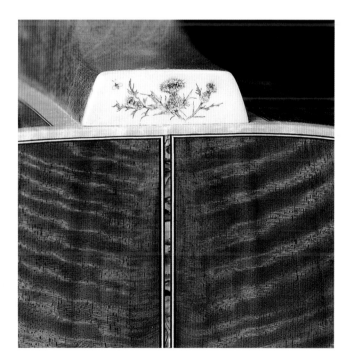

Facing page right and above: **Deluxe Froggy Bottom parlor guitar with walnut body, spruce top, maple binding, slotted headstock, and engraved mammoth ivory heel cap.**

Facing page: **Pimentel and Sons Southwestern concert classical with cutaway and turquoise, coral, and mother-of-pearl inlay.** | Top left: **Rosette on an Oskar Graf C model fingerstyle guitar** *(T.H. Wall Photography).* | Top right: **Heel of an Oskar Graf cutaway** *(T.H. Wall Photography).* | Above: **True North model 1 grand auditorium with salvaged redwood top and curly koa bindings and details.**

Left: **F-style Minstrel 00 with bearclaw Sitka top and custom inlay work.** | Right: **The custom inlays on this Bischoff 2S steel-string include the name of the owner's daughter, Mei Ling, in Chinese characters on the bridge.**

Left: **McCollum Skyforest parlor guitar with custom diamond rosette, abalone top border and fingerboard inlay, and engraved gold Waverly tuners** *(photo by Michael Hoover).* | Right: **Highly figured Brazilian rosewood on the back of a McCollum Skyforest parlor guitar** *(photo by Michael Hoover).*

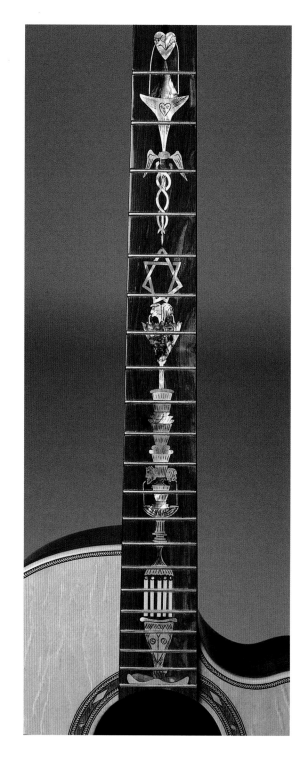

Left: **Bishline flattop with Sitka spruce top, flamed maple binding, and flamed walnut back, sides, and pickguard.** | Right: **Fountain of youth inlay decorating a Timeless GM-03 cutaway.**

Top: **Kim Griffin cutaway with inlaid pickguard.** | Above left: **Doves in flight on a Gibson custom shop special.** | Above right: **Custom Gibson SJ-200 with abalone vine inlay on fingerboard and headstock and engraved pickguard.**

I like to work on instruments for people who play professionally, who push the envelope and push the instruments to the maximum demands of the road. I think the thing that's unique about my instruments is not any one detail or feature, but the experience I bring to the workbench—experience with musicians, and experience gained from being a musician myself. And there is a tremendous amount of information sharing—good, accurate information—within the instrument-building community. As a result, the craft as a whole has improved.

—**Marty Lanham**, Nashville Guitar Co.

Left: **Custom Fylde Goodfellow with Celtic knot inlaid in back.** | Right: **Nashville Guitar Co. 000 12-fret with red spruce top, koa binding, abalone inlay, and pyramid bridge.** | Facing page: **Schoenberg cutaway OM-style Soloist.**

Left: **Rick Turner Expedition model steel-string with floating adjustable neck joint built for world traveler Henry Kaiser.** | Right: **Steve Klein L-45.7 Roses with Kasha-inspired bridge design.**

Top left: **J. Thomas Davis 12-string jumbo with African mahogany back and sides, cedar top, wood purfling and binding, and rose headstock inlay.** | Top right: **Brass and carved-mahogany inlay on a Dave Maize peghead.** | Above: **Huss and Dalton CM custom featuring a drawing of J.E.B. Stuart.**

Left: **Tippin 12-fret 00 with slotted headstock and art deco headstock inlay** *(photo by G. Stahl).* | Right: **Worland parlor guitar with vintage-style inlays.**

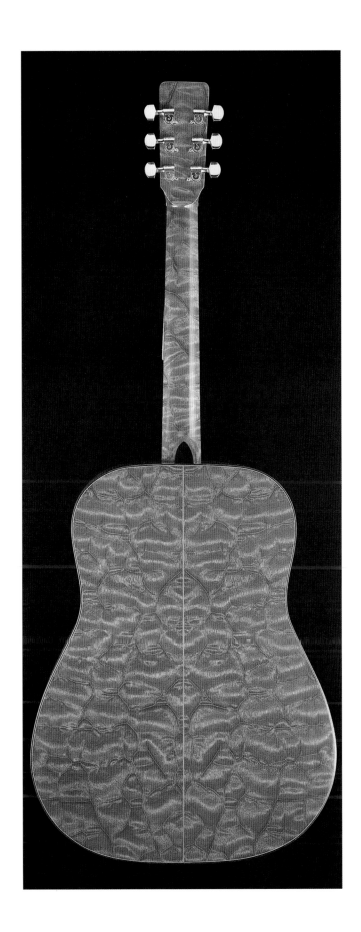

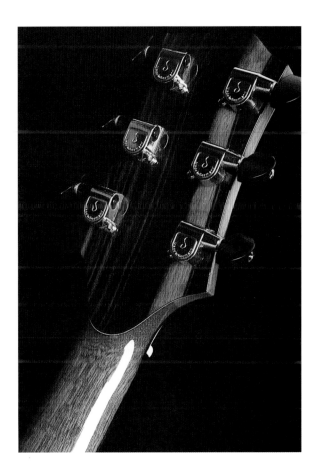

Left: **The back of a Dragge quilted mahogany dreadnought.** | Top right: **Alister Atkin used vintage-style Kluson tuners on this OM-4 headstock.** | Above right: **Macassar ebony on the back of a Kevin Ryan peghead.**

Left: **Double-cutaway Sergei de Jonge steel-string with Engelmann spruce top, ziricote back and sides, and Indian rosewood neck.** | Right: **The Larrivée OM-10 orchestra model with Anna inlay and abalone rosette and purfling.**

I use as many machines as anybody else, if not more. But my hands make the guitar in its entirety; it doesn't take 50 different people. To me, handmade *means smaller production, with one person building it. I don't think that a machine does anything but make the guitar better. Anywhere I can use a machine to replicate something more efficiently and perfectly; that's the object. And most of the time your hands are moving the machine anyway—instead of a chisel, you're moving a router.*

—James Olson

Left: **Olson SJ model with East Indian rosewood body, cedar top, and dove fretboard position markers** *(photo by Dana Wheelock).* | Right: **Custom Schwartz advanced auditorium with Macassar ebony fingerboard and bridge.**

Left: **CFox Sonoma concert model.** | Top right: **Running Dog concert jumbo in American sycamore and Engelmann spruce.** | Above: **OM-style Bristlecone cutaway from Blanchard Guitars with Adirondack spruce top, East Indian rosewood sides, Venetian cutaway, curly koa bindings, and paua abalone rosette** (photo by Steve Soulam).

Right: **Collings Indian/Sitka D3 dreadnought with bound headstock and fretboard, abalone rosette, and gold Waverly tuners.**

Top left: **A Fuller Sound redwood/walnut jumbo with walnut soundhole ring.** | Top right: **Koa and spruce McAlister cutaway.** | Above: **Jamon Zeiler OM-OSH with unusual soundholes.**

Left: **Rosette on a John Mello steel-string cutaway.** | Right: **All-koa Breedlove C22 deep-body concert with sharp cutaway and totem pole fingerboard inlay.**

Top: **Michael Keller jumbo cutaway with abalone fingerboard inlay and mother-of-pearl rosette.** | Above: **Turquoise inlays set off the soundholes in these two Mermer guitars.**

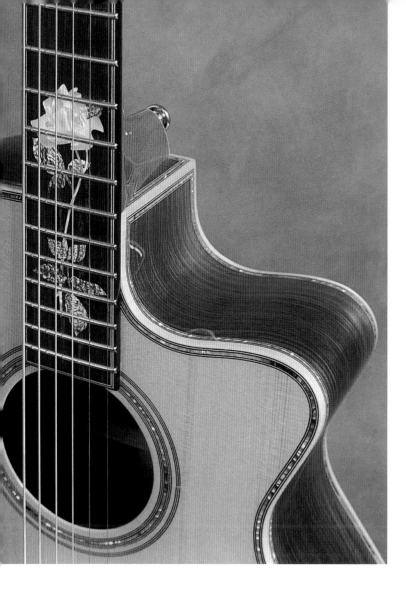

Left: **Rose inlay on a Christopher Melville 000 Presentation.** | Right: **C.F. Martin and Co. transformed a 1968 Brazilian rosewood D-28 into this custom sunburst D-45 conversion model.**

Performers are going to their local makers more than they used to, as evidenced by what they are seen playing on stage and in the media. Our whole culture is shifting values, moving away from overproduced, electric sound. People are tired of it. More often than ever, customers are going to one person to have something built, rather than to an arm's-length retail store.

—**William "Grit" Laskin**

William Laskin used five kinds of stone, three kinds of shell, copper, and walrus ivory in this Kwakiutl tribal mask inlay.

Top left: **Webber Guitars' Blue OM with western big-leaf maple body and Engelmann spruce top.** | Top right: **Steve Grimes Beamer steel-string with double soundholes.** | Above: **Sapphire blue Dillon jumbo thin-body, built for Trisha Yearwood with koa back and sides, Engelmann spruce top, and paua abalone trim.**

Top left: **Queen Shoals jumbo J2.** | Top right: **Louis Hayes steel-string with wooden rosette and pickguard** *(photo by Rory Earnshaw).* | Above: **Doolin double-cutaway steel-string with Indian rosewood back and sides, Sitka spruce top, spalted maple rosette, and pinless bridge.**

Left: **Gallagher auditorium with Brazilian rosewood body, Sitka spruce top, and slotted headstock.** | Right: **Petros Holland Rose D dreadnought with redwood top and rose inlay.**

Nylon-

Strings

Although the six-string guitar was being built and played in most of Europe for almost a century before it caught on in Spain, by the turn of the 20th century the design that evolved in Spain would spread around the world, and many luthiers continue to use it right up until the present day. Seville luthier Antonio de Torres fashioned what would become the definitive form of the guitar, creating a model so superior to its predecessors in power and balance that it could not help but become the standard. Torres selected the best features that several of his contemporaries had been using at the time—fan bracing, a longer scale, a larger soundbox—and fused them with his own bridge design, thus creating a new form that surpassed all others in sonority and projection.

For all of Torres' improvements on the sonority of his instrument, however, the guitar remained locked out of the concert hall because it was still unable to hold its own in the company of symphonic instruments and solo vehicles such as violin and piano. So the guitar remained a fixture only to be heard in the parlors of the elite or on the streets in the hands of common people. Still, some of the greatest classic and Romantic-era composers were enchanted by the sound of the guitar and created a small repertoire of light classical guitar music, which was generally played for friends and associates in informal settings. These charming yet modest pieces by such composers as Beethoven, Sor, Aguado, Carcassi, and Carulli would form the musical foundations for the guitar's future as a full-fledged concert instrument.

When Spanish virtuoso Andrés Segovia performed on the classical guitar in the 1920s, the world at large finally began to respect the instrument and to consider it a "serious" contender for the concert hall. Segovia's course was a difficult one, however. After his 1928 New York debut, a *New York Times* reporter wrote, "Mr. Segovia did not and cannot succeed in removing the limitations which will always surround his instrument. He has stretched these limitations to the utmost. He has far outdistanced in

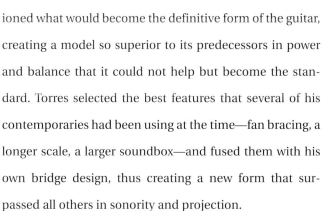

Facing page: **Jim Redgate cedar 2000 concert guitar with Brazilian rosewood sides.** | Above: **Redgate 2000 rosette.**

Top: **Custom rosette with ebony soundhole ring on a Stephan Connor classical** *(photo by Stewart Woodward).* | Above left: **Eric Monrad flamenco with a zero fret, ebony friction pegs, and abalone polka dots on the headstock.** | Above right: **German Vazquez Rubio classical based on a Hauser I.**

his knowledge and his musical conceptions the ordinary twang of strings. Nevertheless, the guitar remains the guitar, with limits of sonority, color, dynamics."

During the following 50 years, Segovia's legendary technique and tone eventually succeeded in earning the guitar the respect of concertgoers around the world, and the Spanish guitar finally became a familiar presence in symphony halls. His style and repertoire were established as the norm, and the classical guitar world also adopted his entrenched conservatism—hence the term *classical* would come to mean strict adherence to the methods and music of the past, a formalism that would brook no experimentation. Even after Segovia's death, the instruments he played, built by such masters as Hauser, Fléta, and Ramírez, became the apotheoses of guitar design. Guitar makers who strayed from these models simply were not taken seriously.

It wasn't until after Segovia's death in 1987 that the world of nylon-string guitars began to expand to include new repertoire, techniques, styles, and eventually new guitar designs. As the classical field became more laid-back, it also became more inviting to players from other realms of the guitar world, expanding the role and the mar-

Left: **A close-up look at the soundhole rosette and pickup controller on a Bischoff Jassical nylon-string** *(photo by Steve Bunck).* | Right: **Dake Traphagen classical.**

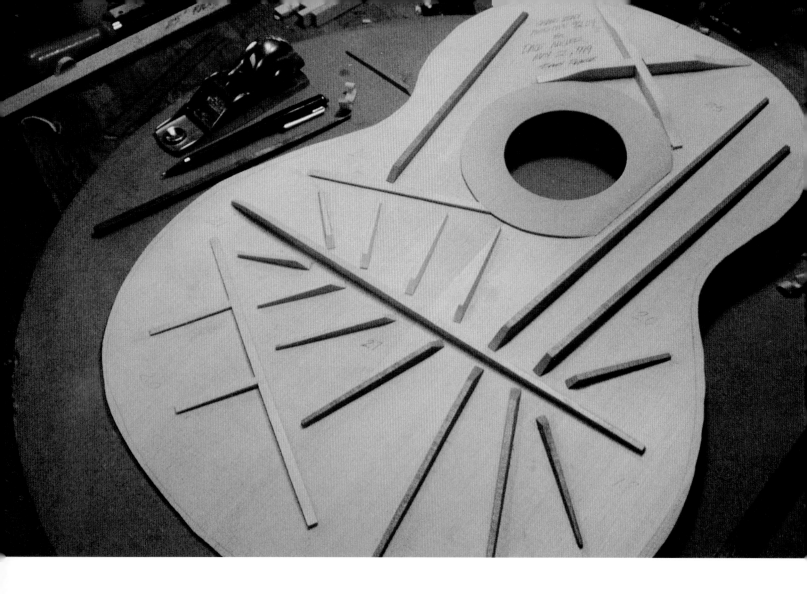

Top: **Kasha-inspired soundboard bracing on a Randy Reynolds Grand Legacy.** | Above: **Robert Ruck concert with acoustic ports in the upper bouts.**

ket for the nylon-string guitar. The instrument made significant inroads into the most unlikely realms. Players like Willie Nelson and Chet Atkins introduced nylon-strings to country-and-western music, while Charlie Byrd championed its use in the jazz world. João Gilberto's bossa nova recordings and Mason Williams' *Classical Gas* even brought the instrument into the Top Ten for a brief period. And yet the nylon-string guitar industry was still

dwarfed by the massive popular interest in steel-string acoustic and electric guitars, and serious players looking for serious nylon-strings were served not by large manufacturers but by individual artisans working in small workshops, including Manuel Velazquez, José Rubio, Michael Gurian, Gene Clark, and Frank Hasselbacher. These dedicated guitar builders made a few dozen instruments per year, predominantly using hand tools, and the instruments were sold in a small number of specialized stores in a just a few cities around the United States. In contrast, the steel-string guitar evolved in the United States as a creature of the industrial revolution, a product of the factory, tailored to the requirements of mass production and mass distribution. And so they've both remained, until recently.

Today, interest in playing and making the nylon-string guitar is greater than it ever has been. Classical guitar is a

Top: **Three-piece Brazilian rosewood back on a David Daily.** | Above: **David Daily classical with 650-mm. scale built for Andrew York.**

I try to learn something with each instrument— something about instrument making, about the materials, and about my craft. That's what makes it worthwhile along the way, because the money isn't the reason to do it, not by itself anyway. I have to be satisfied with having my name on it, and I have to feel that I'm evolving as a builder.

—Jeffrey R. Elliott

Jeffrey R. Elliott concert model constructed in the Torres/Hauser design tradition.

popular college major and doctoral degree. Master classes and recitals are common in virtually every academic setting in the land, where on any given weekend they are filled with prospective young recitalists. The market for nylon-string guitars is rapidly expanding, with players from a wide variety of backgrounds turning to the nylon-string as a source for new colors in their tonal palettes.

Correspondingly, the number of builders serving the market has grown, and nylon-string guitars can now be heard and seen on the radio, television, and even the Internet. The dry, woody sound of the nylon-string guitar lends a fresh, compelling exoticism to Afro-pop, flamenco fusion, the re-emerging Brazilian guitar scene, and even to the performances of such mega-stars as rocker Carlos Santana. The august classical/nylon-string guitar world has let its hair down, so to speak, and today's concert halls are host to classical guitars that are hardly classical in their anatomy, let alone their materials or sound. Experimentation in guitar design and the adoption of new and unusual materials is no longer prohibited. Indeed, each innovation in either the form or structure of the instrument has come to be a factor of great interest and curiosity in the classical guitar community.

Today's neoclassical luthiers are dramatically changing the appearance of their concert instruments. Innovators like Thomas Humphrey, Greg Byers, and Thomas Rein are boldly raising fingerboards off the face of their guitars, which facilitates access to the upper frets and improves tone and sustain in the higher registers. Inside the soundbox, Torres' fan bracing has been replaced with advanced graphite-reinforced, lattice-braced systems with ultrathin tops, low-mass bridges, and massive internal frameworks.

A Blackshear with cedar top and ebony fingerboard.

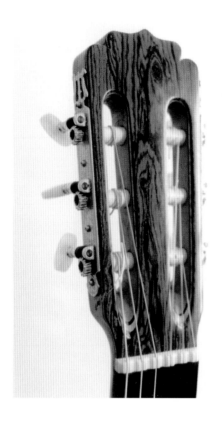
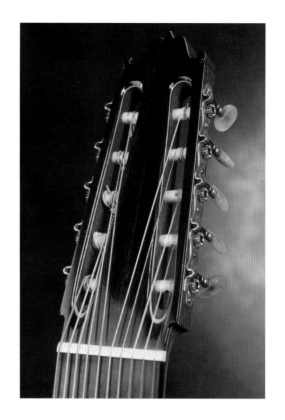

Soundholes are being moved out from under the strings in order to increase the soundboard area. These changes result in instruments with explosive tone and projection (yes, you can now use that adjective to describe the sound of a nylon-string guitar!) when played by the likes of Manuel Barrueco and John Williams. Several prominent nylon-string guitar makers are using lead weights and steel reinforcing bars in their guitars, as well as graphite-reinforced balsa wood braces. Ergonomic body shapes have also become acceptable in the nylon-string world, in response to a growing awareness of guitar-induced injuries. Radical changes in the guitar's anatomy are now the driving motivation not only behind fringe amateurs and experimenting hobbyists but also among renowned makers with firm reputations in their field.

At the same time, there is a large group of luthiers who remain dedicated to the traditional sound and design of the classical guitar. They believe that greater power can only be achieved by sacrificing the warm and intimate tone that defines the classical guitar. Unwilling to make such tradeoffs, these makers are happy to use tried-and-true materials, finishes, and designs to build guitars in the traditional classical form.

The guitar recitalist's traditional sense of inferiority, the age-old result of playing an instrument with an evanescent, perishable sound, is a thing of the past. The nylon-string guitar can now easily hold its own against the piano and even the violin in any concert hall. In the hands of today's bold crop of makers and players, the nylon-string guitar has finally earned the respect and popularity it deserves.

—*William R. Cumpiano*

Left: **Charles Shifflett headstock with scalloped ivory nut.** | Right: **Gamble and O'Toole ebony-bound ten-string headstock.**

The book-matched Brazilian rosewood back of a Sergei de Jonge classical.

Left: **Manzer classical with cedar soundboard, Indian rosewood body, and ebony fingerboard** *(photo by Linda Manzer).* Top right: **Gary Zimnicki Kasha-style model.** | Above right: **A look inside the Coriani Manuel Ramírez 1912 model.**

Top: **Fouilleul Romantic nylon-string based on an 1850s model.** | Above: **Fouilleul Romantic rosette with inlaid burl.**

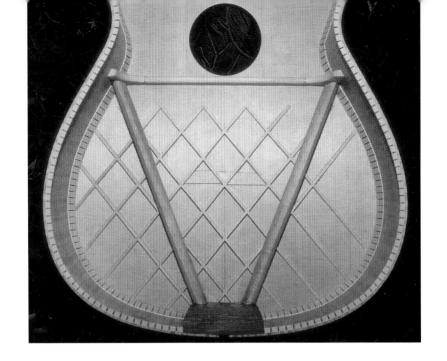

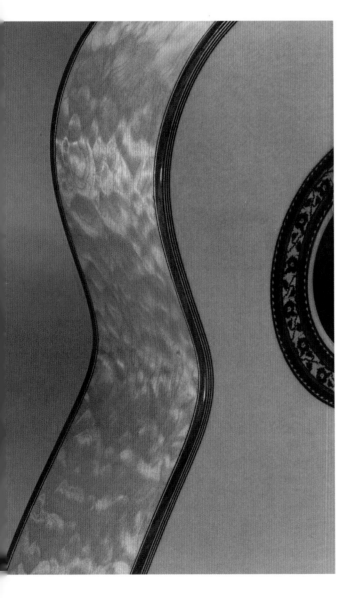

Top: **Lattice bracing and flying braces inside a Buscarino Cabaret nylon-string.** | Above left: **Kenny Hill based this quilted maple classical with German spruce top on the Torres design** *(photo by Paul Schraub).* | Above right: **Miguel Rodriguez–style rosette reproduction by David Schramm.**

I've always felt a freedom of experimentation, a kind of creativity, which is a very American concept. We have no tradition to hold us back, or at least only one that is still in its infancy. When I discuss guitar building with Europeans and Asians, they speak of the tradition of the guitar, but what I see as the tradition of the guitar is its evolution—the fact that it does *change. And the reason it changes is because of the players who are saying, "Give us more."*

—**Thomas Humphrey**

Thomas Humphrey's Millennium model introduced the elevated fingerboard to the classical guitar world.

Left: **Rodriguez C3 flamenco.** | Top right: **Ebony, brown oak, and engraved bone rosette on a Gary Southwell A-series guitar.** | Above right: **Spalted maple rosette on a George Smith classical.**

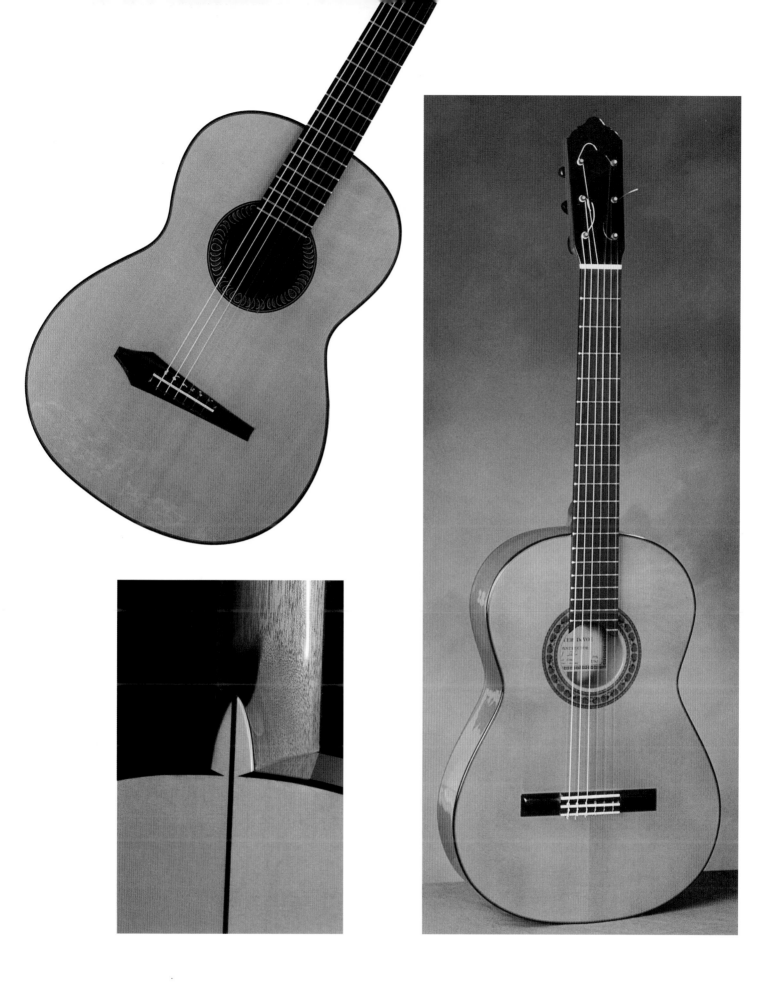

Top left: **Gila Eban's Rochester 1 Centaur.** | Above left: **The heel of a Les Stansell flamenco with ebony binding.** | Above right: **DeVoe traditional flamenco guitar with Spanish cypress back and sides, German spruce top, clear** *golpeador* **(tap plate), and ebony pegs and binding.**

Facing page: **Marc Silber Mestiza Café classic with redwood and western red cedar top** *(photo by Jon Sievert).* | Above left: **A Cumpiano classical with Macassar ebony back and sides and a compression-molded graphite soundboard.** | Above right: **Boaz Clarita Negra concert classical with side soundhole.**

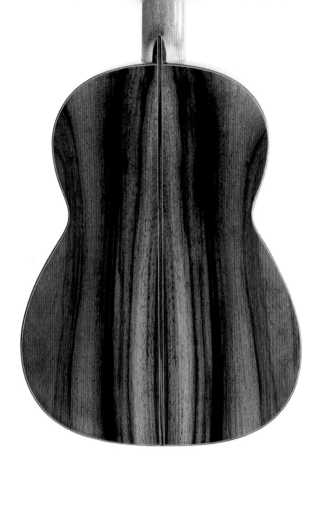

Left: **Brazilian rosewood back of a Shifflett classic.** | Right: **Casa Montalvo concert flamenco with traditional wooden tuning pegs and cypress body.**

Left: **Dennis Hill maple-bodied nylon-string with friction pegs.** | Right: **Madagascar rosewood back on an Aaron Green Concert Negra** *(photo by Stewart Woodward/Visual Talent).*

A r c h t o p s

The acoustic archtop guitar, which lay dormant in recent decades while players favored electric models, has returned to the spotlight. Independent luthiers played a large part in the archtop revival by bringing new energy to an old form. Many of today's top guitar makers build archtops, and inventive designs and decoration often result in instruments that are both musically versatile and highly valued.

Unlike other styles of guitar, the archtop has a distinct lineage and is truly the most American acoustic guitar. Although guitarlike instruments with carved tops and backs were made elsewhere, they appeared to have little influence on Orville Gibson of Kalamazoo, Michigan, whose earliest experiments with violinlike construction for fretted instruments can be traced back to the mid-1890s. Even during a

period in history that saw intense experimentation with musical instruments of all kinds, Gibson's ideas stand out as revolutionary.

Although the soundboards and backs on the earliest Gibson instruments were carved, most of the other features we now associate with archtop guitars were still years away. Orville's guitars had an oval soundhole and pin bridge, with shallow carving of the top and back plates and a low neck angle. Today these instruments look clunky and archaic, but they were radical in their day. The voluptuous curves of the almost round

Facing page: **17-inch Fletcher Brock guitar with Engelmann spruce top, big-leaf maple sides, and ebony fingerboard and tailpiece.** | Above left: **The inlaid ebony headstock on a Jordan.** | Above right: **D'Angelico Excel Deluxe reproduction by Michael Lewis.**

upper and lower bouts, for instance, were a distinct departure from the long, slender guitar shapes popular at the time.

Orville Gibson strung all his instruments with steel strings. In fact, his guitars would have been practically mute with the gut strings used on most guitars of that era. Gibson also made much larger guitars, taking advantage of the greater tension of steel strings. Many of his innovations came from focusing on the mandolin, and for the first 20 years of its existence, the Gibson guitar was primarily an ensemble instrument in mandolin groups.

In 1902, five businessmen from Kalamazoo paid Orville a handsome fee for his patents and his name, and Gibson guitars began to evolve beyond his original plans almost immediately. This included higher arching of the top and back, with steeper neck angles and tailpieces that allowed the use of a high bridge not fastened to the soundboard. Although the round or oval soundhole remained, Gibson guitars slowly began to look more like modern jazz instruments.

But Gibson wouldn't produce an instrument that sounded like a modern jazz guitar until 1922, when the company once again incorporated innovations designed to improve the mandolin. As the mandolin craze in America faded, Gibson's new acoustic engineer, Lloyd Loar, tried to inject excitement into Gibson's faltering sales with a deluxe line of Master Model instruments. The mandolin, mandola, and mandocello style 5 models featured elevated fretboards that didn't touch the top, two s-shaped soundholes, and longer, maple necks that incorporated Gibson's new adjustable steel truss rod. Twin violin-style tone bars ran the length of the top, beneath the feet of the new adjustable bridge. The Gibson F-5s made under Lloyd Loar's influence are now considered the finest archtop mandolins every produced.

Loar gave Gibson's largest guitar of that period a similar treatment. By eliminating the round soundhole between the bridge and the fretboard, the guitar's bridge could be moved closer to the neck block, allowing a neck with 14 frets clear of the body. The bridge sat in the center of a soundboard now free to vibrate across its entire surface. This was the first truly modern archtop guitar. Unfortunately Loar left Gibson barely two years later, after only a few dozen of the new L-5s had been produced.

While Loar's innovations for the mandolin came too late, his new guitar design was almost ahead of its time.

17-inch D'Leco Legacy L-17 with Macassar trim and tailpiece.

America was in the midst of the roaring '20s, and a new music called jazz was sweeping the country (though it wasn't what we call jazz today). The four-string banjo had been driving the rhythm section in dance bands, but as bandleaders added more vocals and slower numbers to their repertoire, a smoother, more versatile sound was needed. The sweetness of a guitar's tone was ideal, but even with steel strings a flattop guitar just wasn't loud enough. The new L-5 offered lots more volume and better access to the upper frets as well. In the hands of players like Eddie Lang, the guitar's potential as a solo instrument opened new vistas. By the late 1920s, the Gibson L-5 was

Left: **Mortoro Starling with bird-shaped soundholes.** | Right: **Mark Lacey Virtuoso with black lacquer finish and engraved tailpiece.**

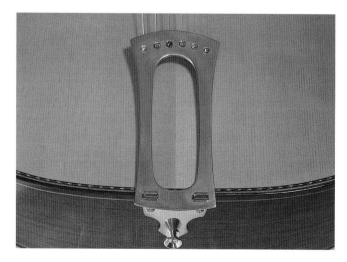

Left: **Schröder Concordia Excel with European spruce top and highly figured maple body.** | Top right: **Mark Campellone model with Sitka spruce top, figured maple body, multiple binding, and special tailpiece.** | Above right: **Two-piece brass tailpiece on a Stefan Sobell model 1.**

found on bandstands and in recording studios from coast to coast.

Even today, many studio guitarists would argue that if the development of the archtop guitar had stopped with the 1929 L-5, they would be content. But the success of Gibson's L-5 spawned a number of imitations, and in the 1930s a typical American combination of innovation and competition produced a dizzying sequence of changes to the archtop guitar.

Epiphone introduced an entire line of f-hole archtops in 1931, and Gibson followed suit in 1932. The $250 L-5 was clearly too expensive for all but the most serious and well-paid guitarists, especially during the Depression. Soon similar but plainer models, such as Gibson's L-7, were introduced at half that price. By this time archtops were America's favorite, and every guitar manufacturer, including Martin, was offering them.

Despite greatly improved projection compared to flat-top guitars, even the L-5 was outgunned on the bandstand by louder instruments. In the days before guitars could be effectively amplified electrically, Gibson answered the call for more volume the only way it could, with bigger guitars. In late 1934 the L-5 was introduced in a new, 17-inch-wide Advanced model, but this dramatic change was almost eclipsed by the Super 400, a new 18-inch model that used one of Orville Gibson's long-abandoned guitar shapes. This new behemoth was lavishly decorated with multiple black and white lines bordering every edge, and the bold, split-block neck inlays gave it an art-deco gleam. Gibson had competitors on its heels almost immediately, but with the new L-5 and Super 400, the company had taken charge of the archtop guitar market.

The final bit of archtop evolution was the addition of a cutaway in the upper bout, which allowed easy access to even the highest strings. Gibson first offered this option in 1939, and that same year customers were also offered the choice of a gleaming natural finish. By now, big companies like Epiphone and Gretsch weren't the only ones offering jazz-age guitarists an alternative. Smaller shops like that of John D'Angelico of New York and Elmer Stromberg of Boston offered

Top: **Ebony and ivory inlay work on the back of a curly maple Petillo.** | Above: **Engraved tailpiece and rhodium plating on Zeidler's blue Jazz Deluxe Special, made for the Chinery collection.**

When I find better ways to build, I use them. It's easy to get hung up on time-honored building techniques, but to do so is to forget the goal: creating the best guitar possible.

—Robert Benedetto

Robert Benedetto's La Cremona Azzurra features a solid ebony tailpiece and simple appointments *(photo by Leslie Jean-Bart).*

handmade archtops of the highest quality, adding stylistic flourishes uniquely their own.

Gibson's archtop guitar production was severely affected by World War II, and by the time the company could once again focus on musical instruments, it no longer sought to spur guitar sales with new developments in acoustic guitars. When guitar production resumed after the war, the emphasis was on amplified tone, not acoustic volume.

The acoustic archtop was far from dead, even if it no longer ruled the catalog covers of major manufacturers. Gibson continued to sell both acoustic and amplified versions of the Super 400 and the L-5, along with less expensive versions like the ever-popular L-7. Stromberg and D'Angelico continued doing what they did best, largely ignoring the call to amplify their instruments. John D'Angelico's creations continued to evolve, and his 18-inch New Yorker and 17-inch Excel models are now considered high points in archtop guitar design.

Left: **Ted Megas 17-inch sunburst Athena, with Sitka spruce top, flamed maple body, and white binding.** | Right: **Seven-string Tom Ribbecke Monterey acoustic-electric with ebony pickguard and custom tailpiece and finish** *(Youngblood Photography).*

The good times for acoustic archtops couldn't last, however. Gibson acquired the faltering Epiphone company in the mid-1950s, around the same time Elmer Stromberg died, and as that decade ended, the acoustic archtop was getting little nurturing from Gibson. As long as the big humbucking pickups in the top functioned properly, most of Gibson's archtop guitar customers were content. After all, a highly responsive archtop just becomes a feedback demon when plugged in and played at high volume.

In the early 1950s, John D'Angelico hired 17-year-old James D'Aquisto, an apprentice who would prove to be the single tenuous link to the original jazz-age giants of the archtop guitar. After D'Angelico's untimely death in 1964, D'Aquisto continued to build the New Yorker and Excel models under his own name. By the 1970s, he had further

Left: **Steve Andersen Model 17 with Adirondack spruce top, curly maple body, violin finish, and Armstrong floating pickup.** | Right: **The body of a 16-inch Andersen oval-hole archtop with Engelmann spruce top and curly maple sides.**

Left: **Comins 17-inch Chester Avenue model.** | Top right: **17-inch Jazz Reflections archtop by Bill Hollenbeck.** | Above right: **Ric McCurdy Moderna Classic made with quilted maple, ebony, and Sitka spruce.**

refined them with his unique style. As younger builders entered the field, D'Aquisto served as a strong mentor, pointing the way with his new Classic models, which featured a clean, minimalist design. D'Aquisto's bold innovations combined with his direct link to the past make him stand out as perhaps the greatest champion of the acoustic archtop guitar.

A custom archtop guitar offers the sophisticated purchaser many advantages. Guitarists had a limited number of tonal options 60 years ago. Today, archtop guitars are just as likely to be used for subtle chord voicings as for socking out rhythm chops, and the owner's needs can be accommodated by a sensitive builder. The thickness, bracing, and even the species of spruce used for the top, for

Left: **Napolitano Primavera inspired by the work of John D'Angelico.** | Right: **J. Thomas Davis archtop with European spruce top and walnut pickguard.**

instance, can be altered to better suit the intended string gauge and playing style. And while neck widths and overall shape used to fall within a narrow range regardless of who made the guitar, today's builders can easily accommodate a player's small hands or desire for different string spacing.

Besides the obvious options in binding and inlay, most modern builders also have a much wider range of woods and finishes to choose from than was available in decades past. Do you prefer your maple quilted or with a fiddle-back pattern? Violin-style shading, vintage sunburst, or natural coloring? Glossy finish or satin? As these pages indicate, there has never been such a wealth of choices—in both materials and builders—for those interested in owning an archtop guitar.

—*Richard Johnston*

Left: **A 17-inch Marchione with Engelmann spruce top, quilted maple body, ebony pickguard, and floating neck extension.** | Right: **Zeidler Jazz Deluxe Special with tortoiseshell pickguard and tailpiece.**

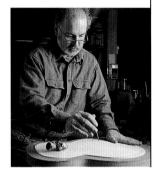

Not much is really known about the effect of the instrument's sides on the sound. That goes for violin, guitar...anything. I do know that the structural integrity between the top and back at the side's juncture is extremely important. You cannot sacrifice that edge and allow it to be detached. A perfect example is an older guitar where the glue seam has let go on that side edge. The instrument loses 70 percent of its sound. It's like short-circuiting the soundboard.

—John Monteleone

Monteleone Grand Artist with triport design, 18-inch scroll body, German spruce top, big-leaf maple body and neck, curly maple binding, and Macassar ebony appointments.

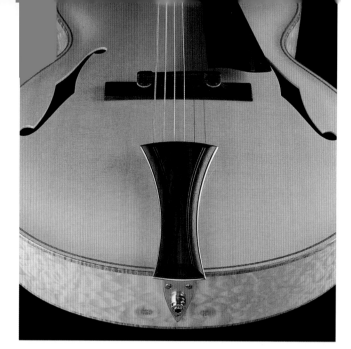

Left: **16-inch De Paule Jazzman with custom Florentine soundholes, tiger-striped maple sides, and mother-of-pearl inlays.** | Top right: **Ted Megas Appollo tailpiece.** | Above right: **Steve Grimes Montreux with European curly maple body, German spruce top, and ebony fingerboard, pickguard, and tailpiece.**

17-inch Hemken with wood bindings and ebony appointments.

Top left: **Brad Nickerson 17-inch Virtuoso with European spruce top and wood binding.** | Top right: **Taku Sakashta's 17-inch Karizma with engraved ebony tailpiece and Kent Armstrong pickup.** | Above: **Buscarino Monarch with sunburst finish, flamed maple body, and tree-of-life fingerboard inlay.**

Resonat

ors and
Hawaiians

When Christopher Knutsen and Hermann Weissenborn, innovators of the hollow-neck Hawaiian steel, and brothers John and Rudy Dopyera, geniuses behind National and Dobro resonator guitars, were developing their respective creations, their primary purpose was to create guitars with greater volume. But the reason these instruments are still cherished and copied 80 years later is because of their unique tone. And for a new generation of instrument makers, improving on some of the original resonator and Hawaiian guitars is a formidable challenge.

Knutsen, Weissenborn, and the Dopyera brothers seem to have gotten it right with their respective instruments almost from the start. While there was surely more trial and error than history recalls, the short time frames in which these instruments evolved is testimony to the genius of these makers. And the many astounding ways that guitar players use the instruments contributes to their renaissance and ever-growing popularity.

Guitarists everywhere, from the Mississippi Delta to the jazz salons of Paris, owe a

Facing page: **Beltona Triple Resonator with nickel-plated brass body, ebony fingerboard, and pearloid headstock.** | Above left: **Joseph Yanuziello square-neck resophonic with curly maple body, fire chief finish, and black-and-white stitch purfling.** | Above right: **Manzanita H hollow-neck Hawaiian guitar with Sitka spruce top and Indian rosewood back and sides.**

big debt to Hawaiians and South American cowboys of the late 1800s, who were invited by King Kamehameha to remedy the islands' cattle overpopulation problem. They brought their stringed instruments and even left some behind—but the native Hawaiians had no idea how to play them. They soon discovered open chords and developed what is today known as the slack-key style.

Another quantum leap occurred when young Joseph Kekuku accidentally dropped a comb or knife on the strings of a guitar (although his responsibility for the technique is disputed in some circles). He liked what he heard and started experimenting with using a metallic object to substitute for the left-hand fingering. This technique had about a generation to evolve before Hawaiian music swept the mainland like wildfire, ignited by the spark of the 1915 Panama-Pacific Exposition in San Francisco. Steel guitar had always involved a standard instrument played flat on the lap with the strings raised above the fretboard. As the popularity of

Hawaiian music grew, someone—probably Chris Knutsen—had the inspiration to adapt a guitar exclusively for Hawaiian playing. These basic improvements included flush fret markers, a built-in high nut, and a body chamber extending up the neck.

Hermann Weissenborn made similar-looking instruments, but with improvements that included superior construction (he seems to have been alone among hollow-neck makers in adapting the Martin X-brace design) and consistency in manufacturing. Weissenborn's lines of Hawaiian and Spanish guitars each have four styles of trim, from very plain to extensively rope-bound. These styles (mostly) carried over to the Kona line of Hawaiian guitars made by Weissenborn for Los Angeles teacher and publisher C.S. DeLano.

The next big advance came from brothers John and Rudy Dopyera (the latter worked for Weissenborn at one time) in the form of their mechanical-resonator National

Jerry Timm square-neck resonator with nontraditional soundholes and fret markers.

Top left: **National Reso-Phonic '59 Fins tricone, with nickel-plated brass body and '50s-era engravings.** | Above left: **National Reso-Phonic custom Chrysanthemum tricone with style 4 engravings, mother-of-pearl fingerboard inlays, and basket-weave grilles.** | Above right: **Fine Resophonic's nickel-plated style III resonator with single cone, 14-fret neck, and engraved ivy leaves.**

guitars. The tricone emerged initially as a Hawaiian instrument after the Dopyeras were approached by vaudeville performer George Beauchamp. John Dopyera used hard, thin resonating cones to translate a guitar's string movement into greater volume, which worked much the way a speaker does. Dopyera experimented with one to four cones and settled on three as optimal, and he used an aluminum alloy for spinning cones on a lathe. Nationals were an immediate hit.

But despite the success of the guitars, there was deep discord among National's principals, and John and Rudy Dopyera left the company in 1928 and formed Dobro. They came up with a new wood-body, single-cone design that didn't infringe on the patents they'd signed over to National. But the differences between Nationals and Dobros run deeper than just whether the bodies are made of steel or wood. The distinction is actually internal—in the style of

Left: **John Reuter round-neck resonator with Florentine cutaway and highly figured koa top, back, and sides.** | Right: **Randy Allen square-neck resophonic with figured maple body, engraved resonator coverplate, and shell inlays.**

cones each employs. National cones in both the tricone and single-cone designs are convex with respect to the guitar top. Dobro resonators are bowl-shaped, raised in the center, and spanned by a cast aluminum "spider" with a bridge in the center and eight legs resting on the perimeter of the cone.

Dobros were mostly built out of laminated wood, since the Dopyeras thought the resonator was key to the sound and that the body was more of a supporting than a resonating structure. This meant that Dobros could be sold at a fraction of the price of Nationals, which would prove essential to survival during the Depression. National answered with its own single-resonator designs—the German silver Don model, styles O and N (brass), and the workmanlike Triolian and Duolian (whose punchy, steel-bodied sound has become the signature tone of budget-conscious blues belters), as well as a few wood-body guitars.

In the years leading up to World War II, small improvements were made to resonator and Hawaiian designs, but there were no breakthrough innovations. World War II put the brakes on all but a few musical instruments as America directed its manufacturing base to the war effort. After the war, production of resonator instruments was history. Electric guitars were the new reigning monarchy.

From the '40s into the '60s, resonator and hollow-neck Hawaiian guitars became ancient curiosities or else dark matter occupying deep spaces in closets, attics, and dusty places under beds. A few die-hard blues aficionados kept the National blues/bottleneck tradition alive, while in country and bluegrass music, two players kept the Dobro from going the way of the dodo: Beecher "Pete" Kirby (aka

Top: **Curly maple Scheerhorn L-Body square-neck resonator.** | Bottom: **The Del Vecchio–inspired McGill resonator guitar with cedar top and Indian rosewood back and sides.**

I'm not like most of the builders today. I'm from the old school. I still build out of ply. I find that I can get more tone and volume from it than from anything else. I know that the standard has been to build out of solid wood, but you have to keep in mind that when you build a resonator guitar you cut a hole in the top to accommodate the cone and spider, and that means you're removing most of the soundboard! So I think that you have to consider a resonator guitar almost like you do a speaker cabinet.

—Ivan Guernsey

Bashful Brother Oswald), who played with Roy Acuff, and Burkett "Josh" Graves, who played with Flatt and Scruggs. Their recorded work stimulated new generations of virtuosos, including Mike Auldridge, Jerry Douglas, and a legion of disciples.

Rudy and brother Ed Dopyera—and for a while, the Mosrite company—made some Dobros in the '60s. After Mosrite shut down, the Dopyeras ultimately got the Dobro name back and in 1970 formed Original Musical Instruments, which was virtually the only maker of res-

onator guitars for two decades. Gibson bought OMI in 1993, then relocated production to Nashville in 1997.

Nationals' return to favor can be partially credited to virtuoso Bob Brozman and his obsession with National instruments and the music they made in their heyday—Hawaiian, jazz, calypso, and blues. In 1985, Nationals went from obscure esoteric to hip mainstream when Dire Straits put Mark Knopfler's late-'30s style O on the cover of their multi-million-selling *Brothers in Arms* album. Prices surged dramatically almost overnight for National metal-bodies and suddenly a new market presented itself.

Left: **Scheerhorn L-Body square-neck resonator with spruce top and curly koa binding.** | Right: **Mermer Maalea Weissenborn-style slide guitar with koa body and dual offset soundholes.**

Don Young had been working off and on for OMI/ Dobro since the early '70s, when he decided to strike out on his own. He and partner MacGregor Gaines began National Reso-Phonic in 1988 as a two-man operation building wood-body guitars. They added a single-cone style O reproduction in 1992 and then round-neck tricones.

Although he'd been playing them for years by the time players started taking notice in the late '80s, David Lindley almost single-handedly brought Weissenborns back to the attention of other players. Assists can be credited to Ry Cooder and Steve Fishell, who used Weissenborns in his stint with Emmylou Harris' Hot Band. And close examination of a couple of John Fahey's albums reveals a Kona style 3.

With renewed interest in these instruments, new demand was far in excess of the diminished vintage supply. Today, individual custom luthiers as well as huge offshore factories are making unprecedented numbers of Weissenborn-, National-, and Dobro-inspired instruments.

Interestingly, the proliferation of offshore Regals, Johnsons, and Epiphones hasn't hurt the high-end builders. "That's actually a good thing for me," says Tim Scheerhorn. "When people buy these beginner instruments, they're going to want something high-end and custom when they become accomplished."

Perhaps because of the lack of metal fabrication involved, more modern-day luthiers seem to be trying their hands at making Weissenborn-style Hawaiians. Among the elegant re-creations on the market are the traditionally styled Bear Creek instruments, the distinctively Deco Hawaiian King by Toronto luthier Joseph Yanuziello,

Bear Creek's koa HN-AC hollow-neck Hawaiian with rope binding.

and the double-soundhole Mermer Maalea. Marc Silber's Mexican-manufactured hollow-necks carry a budget price—and the endorsement of David Lindley, who uses them on the road, leaving his vintage originals safe at home.

A revival of the tricone guitar was slower to materialize because of the daunting tooling expenses involved. Nevertheless, Continental tricones were imported by Saga in the early '90s and were joined in the market by British Beltonas (first made in Britain and now in New Zealand), National Reso-Phonics, and Johnsons. Still, modern-day tricones are made of plated brass rather than the original (and prohibitive) German silver. Fine Resophonic has bridged the tricone with its hollow-neck Hawaiian forebears (or Dobro descendants) by making a tricone with a laminated maple body. In the late '70s, Oklahoma builder Rudy Q. Jones made some solid-wood resophonics that were used by Jerry Douglas and Josh Graves. Jones eschewed the traditional circular soundwell that surrounds the cone in favor of internal baffles, setting the stage for other makers like Tim Scheerhorn, who has embraced solid-wood body construction while using other nontraditional notions in internal structure.

As you can see in these pages, these aren't your granddaddy's Weissenborns or resonators. The golden age of lutherie has brought myriad improvements, both audio and visual, to designs that were pretty darn good to begin with.

—Ben Elder

Facing page: **Joseph Yanuziello Hawaiian King Special hollow-neck with curly koa body.** | Above: **Silber Hawaiian Model 4 Plus with hollow neck and all solid woods** *(photo by Jon Sievert).*

Specialty

Guitars

Musicians in the 21st century have many styles of guitar at their disposal—dreadnoughts, parlor guitars, classicals, archtops, resonators—but for some, standard models and designs, even those that have been custom-tweaked, cannot supply the sounds that match their musical visions. These are the people who are driving custom guitar makers forward in their development of the unusual, the rare, and the downright bizarre! They seek instruments that expand the available sonic palette, that imitate the tones of ancient guitars, or that allow them to compose and play the music they hear in their minds—music that cannot be produced on "normal" guitars. There are no limitations to luthiers' imaginations, and many of the designs that they discover when building one-of-a-kind guitars prove useful in their more standard models.

In many cases, these specialty guitars are true collaborations between the player and the luthier. Linda Manzer, for example, could not have completed the Pikasso guitar without hands-on advice from the player for whom she built it, Pat Metheny, and they went on to work together on such unique creations as a sitar-guitar and a nylon-string archtop. Likewise, Alex de Grassi's Sympitar, created by luthier Fred Carlson, was very much a collaborative effort. Both instruments are radical departures from traditional design, yet anyone who has heard Metheny or de Grassi play these instruments can attest to the

Facing page: **Multilayered parchment rosette in an R.E. Bruné Baroque.** | Above left: **The tailpiece, bridge, and D-shaped soundhole of a Shelley Park Elan** (Ken Barbour Photography). | Above right: **An eight-string Ganz classical with Engelmann spruce top.**

success of the experiments. When eclectic guitarist Henry Kaiser decided to record an album in Antarctica, he needed to commission an instrument that could withstand extreme temperatures and the rigors of traveling by dogsled. Kaiser turned to luthier Rick Turner, who built him a carbon fiber–reinforced guitar with interchangeable necks for baritone and standard scale lengths.

Sometimes the special needs of a player are simpler, involving, for example, a different tonal range. Baritone guitars fall into the deliciously rumbling spectrum between a standard guitar and a bass. They feature a longer scale (generally between 26 and 28 inches) and are tuned anywhere from one to four whole steps below standard tuning. Baritones are garnering attention from players of all musical styles, and many luthiers are now offering their own unique takes on them.

Left: **Shelley Park Encore in Brazilian rosewood and German spruce** (Ken Barbour Photography). | Right: **Novax A-X seven-string acoustic-electric with carved, arched spruce top, maple back and sides, and the Novax fanned fretboard.**

In some cases, six strings just aren't enough. Seven-string guitars are the current craze in the realm of electrics, and in the nylon-string world, artists are using such many-stringed beasts as Charles Vega's finely crafted ten-string classical. The late Michael Hedges brought the harp guitar back into vogue, and his performance ax of choice was a one-of-a-kind electric creation built by Steve Klein. Other builders, including Ralph Bown and Lance McCollum, are creating modern adaptations of the acoustic harp guitars popular in the early 1900s. Archtop builders and players are also coming down with multiple-string fever. Ralph Novak built an eight-string archtop for jazz sensation Charlie Hunter and also offers a more manageable seven-string version. His multiple-string archtops, and others like it, extend the range of a standard guitar (most often with an

Left: **Beyond the Trees Harpeggione with carved redwood top and maple tailpiece.** | Right: **The Rick Turner Mando-Guitar with scaled-down 1934 Super 400 body and Ralph Novak fanned fingerboard is tuned F C G D A E (low to high).**

extra low bass string tuned to A or B) and are helping to redefine the role of the guitar in jazz accompaniment.

Selmer/Maccaferri-style guitars are only available from individual makers and smaller manufacturers. Without these unique instruments, acoustic swingers emulating the work of Django Reinhardt and the Hot Club of France would be unable to do their thing. Luthiers like Michael Dunn, Shelley Park, and John Le Voi, as well as small man-

Left: **William Eaton seven-string vihuela with ibinza wood and mother-of-pearl inlays.** | Right: **Custom Ovation six/12 double-neck built for Richie Sambora.**
Facing page: **Dyer-style harp guitar by Ralph Bown.**

Front and back views of a 1977 R.E. Bruné Baroque guitar based on a Voboam instrument with tied gut frets built in the late 1600s.

ufacturers like Dell'Arte and Guitares Maurice Dupont, offer precise replicas of the original Selmer and Maccaferri guitars as well as adaptations for modern players. Some artists find their niche playing classical music on authentic period-style

instruments. Several luthiers, including Richard Bruné, have responded by re-creating the predecessors to the modern Torres-style nylon-string guitar. Such guitars offer museum-quality looks and construction but are not too fragile to be used as working instruments.

It is clear that there are many reasons for ordering a specialty guitar. And who knows what kinds of creative opportunities some of these one-of-a-kind instruments and vintage replicas will make possible? The spirit of innovation and invention that goes into specialty guitars like the ones pictured here is just the kind of energy that created the golden age of lutherie that we've all been enjoying for the past ten or 20 years.

—Teja Gerken

Top: **D soundhole inlay detail on a Le Voi Maccaferri-style.** | Above: **Linda Manzer built the Pikasso, a 42-stringed harp guitar with full MIDI capabilities, for jazz artist Pat Metheny** (photo by Brian Pickell).

I was fascinated by the music of Django Reinhardt—and even more fascinated when I found out about these peculiar guitars. I go for as much volume as I can possibly extract out of an instrument. The tone will develop, it will mellow—and the player can control the sound of a bright instrument with right-hand technique. My job as an instrument maker is to make the guitar responsive and balanced. The sound is what the musician does to it, not me. I've got to make it so that in the hands of five different players, it might very well sound five different ways.
—**Michael Dunn**

Selmer-style Dunn Belleville with cedar top and rosewood back and sides.

Left: **The Charles Vega 11-string Guitarra Téorba combines elements of the Baroque lute with the classical guitar.** | Right: Dell'Arte Swing 42 **inspired by a 1950s Joseph DiMauro guitar.**

Shopping for a
Custom Guitar

Julie Bergman

Buying a custom-made guitar can be one of the most rewarding experiences you'll ever have in your musical lifetime. Players buy custom instruments for different reasons. They seek specific woods or construction options not available in off-the-shelf models, or they just want to take part in the creation of their future musical partner. Whatever your reason for commissioning a guitar, you'll need to put a great deal of thought and planning into the project and to communicate clearly with the luthier you choose.

CHOOSING A BUILDER

Different builders specialize in different kinds of instruments: acoustic steel-strings, classicals, archtops, harp guitars, etc. As you narrow your search, be sure that the builders you're considering actually make the kind of instrument you want. It's pointless to seek out the world's most renowned archtop builder and then order a classical guitar. Once you've identified an appropriate luthier whose work you admire and whose guitars are in your price range,

see if it's possible to play one or more of the builder's guitars. Your odds may depend on whether or not you live near a major metropolitan area, but the listings at the back of this book (see page 122) include luthiers from all over the United States, as well as Canada and Europe. You may want to start your research by finding out whose guitars your favorite players use. Some publications, including *Acoustic Guitar*, provide that information when they profile an artist. You should also browse builders' sites on the Web (www.acousticguitar.com provides hundreds of links) and haunt the best acoustic guitar shops in your area. The instrument you're looking for may not be hanging on the shop's wall, but one of the employees might own one and be willing to bring it in for an in-store trial. Or the maker may be willing to set you up with a previous customer in your area, who will let you play his or her instrument. There may even be an upcoming guitar exhibition or music festival in your area that features samples of a particular builder's work.

SELECTING OPTIONS

Some of the decisions you'll have to make include body size, neck shape, woods, scale length, and whether or not to include an internal pickup. Most of these decisions

Steve Grimes shaves an archtop brace (photo by Ingrid Overgard).

Julie Bergman's Kevin Ryan guitar in progress.

depend on how you intend to use the instrument (at home, on stage, in the studio) and what type of music you play. Smaller-bodied instruments, often termed orchestra models (OMs) or grand concert models, are as popular today as the larger-bodied dreadnought developed by C.F. Martin and Co. years ago. Traditional dreadnoughts are loud and powerful with a tremendous bass response, while smaller-bodied guitars can offer a more precise, balanced sound that is often sought for recording situations. The size of the body will also affect the gauge of strings you need to use. Light-gauge steel strings, for example, are usually recommended for small-bodied flattops. Specific needs may send you to a builder known for a particular specialty, or you may prefer to work with a luthier open to a wide variety of construction options, woods, bodies, and styles.

The conversation between you and the builder, store employee, or dealer will start with these factors and then branch off into the finer details, such as the shape of the body, the dimensions of the neck, the price, what kind of deposit you need to put down, how long you'll have to wait for the finished guitar, and the warranty terms. A luthier's construction techniques, such as internal bracing patterns and finish, are usually static, so if you have strong preferences about them, you should take that into account when choosing a builder. Many luthiers and shops will do sunburst or tinted finishes, but they usually charge significantly more for them.

Whether or not you order a cutaway will depend on how far up the neck you tend to play. While some builders feel that cutaways affect the sound of the guitar, others believe that they cause no loss of volume or tone. Most builders and shops will also accommodate left-handed players with custom cutaways.

When it comes to scale length, most luthiers will honor requests for slight variations on what they normally use. These days, it's almost as easy to order a guitar with 12 frets clear of the body as it is to order a 14-fret guitar. Some flattop builders, including Kevin Ryan, are using slightly longer scale lengths (25.7 inches as opposed to 25.5) to increase the string tension slightly and thus accommodate lowered open tunings. Archtop and flattop builders may opt for a scale length of 24.75, 25, or 25.4 inches, depending on the type of guitar, and the scale for parlor guitars can be even shorter.

As far as choosing tonewoods is concerned, you'll need to decide on woods for the soundboard, the back and sides, the neck (although mahogany is by far the most common choice), the fretboard, and the headstock veneer. Ebony is the most common fretboard wood, but various types of rosewood can also be used.

Bindings and purfling are frequently chosen by the buyer, and most makers offer the option to bind the neck and headstock in addition to the body of the guitar. Ivoroid (or other synthetic materials such as fake tortoiseshell) used to be the most common binding, but more and more high-end luthiers are turning to wood. Ivoroid bindings may be easier to repair, and they offer a more traditional look on archtops and certain vintage-style flattops. Herringbone and abalone edge inlays are commonly available, although they'll add to the cost of your guitar.

Other options include the type of headstock (solid versus slotted) and sometimes its shape, the tuners (silver- or gold-plated, for example), the rosette design, the type of pickguard (tortoiseshell, clear plastic, wood, floating), fingerboard and/or headstock inlays, and other cosmetic touches.

Some luthiers do their own inlay work, while others hire specialists like Larry Robinson. Intricate inlay work is hugely time-consuming and will cost you, but a unique (tasteful) design can add to your guitar's value. Many builders will create an inlay based on your original sketch. A less costly option is to choose from among several inlay designs the maker cuts via a CNC (computer numerically controlled) design. Keep in mind that inlaying your name into the instrument will make it almost impossible to resell.

NECK SPECS

After the neck and fingerboard woods are chosen, the measurements of the neck need to be pinned down. The neck connects the player to the instrument, and defining its dimensions is one of the most important factors in ordering a comfortable guitar. The size of your hands and your playing style are the two most important factors to consider. You may be most comfortable with the neck of the instrument you learned on, and it's quite common for a customer to bring a luthier his or her favorite guitar and request that the neck be replicated for the new instrument.

The neck width (the distance from side to side) is usually measured at the nut, and it also affects string spacing. Many vintage guitars sport a $1^{11}\!/_{16}$-inch nut width, which is also commonly used on electric guitar necks. Builders catering to fingerstyle players frequently ship with a $1\frac{3}{4}$-inch nut width but will go wider or thinner upon request. Some major manufacturers tend toward the $1^{11}\!/_{16}$-inch nut for dreadnought bodies and the $1\frac{3}{4}$-inch width for orchestra model guitars. The necks on classical guitars are much wider, normally about two inches at the nut.

The neck profile, also referred to as the depth or thickness, is the distance from front to back. Some players prefer a fatter neck, while others like a thin or "fast" neck. The shape can vary from an oval or C shape to a V shape. Another question is how the neck is joined to the body. In the past, dovetail joints were the only acceptable ones in quality guitars, but today many builders use bolt-on necks.

Metal truss rods are common in steel-string guitars, and many builders are using a combination of a truss rod and carbon graphite for added strength and stability. The neck on an instrument with no truss rod cannot be easily adjusted in response to humidity changes or long-term change brought on by string tension.

TERMS AND FINANCES

After you've nailed down all the specs and design options, it's time to discuss payment and warranty terms. In some cases, the luthier's waiting list is so long that he or she cannot guarantee the price of the instrument. The cost of woods and supplies is always rising, and the maker's current price may not be enough to cover costs and make a profit five years up the road. Ask what happens if you don't like the finished product. Will the luthier sell it to someone else and start from scratch on a new instrument for you? Will he or she make alterations to the guitar, and if so, will you have to pay extra? Can you get a full refund of your deposit? It's best to get such policies in writing before you pay your deposit. Also find out how long you can expect to wait for your guitar. Estimates for turnaround times can be found on the *Acoustic Guitar* Web site at www.acousticguitar.com, but workloads and backlogs are always changing, so it's a good idea to ask.

Because of the subtle variations in woods (even from the same tree), the tonal qualities of a guitar can never be fully anticipated in advance. If the sound of the finished instrument is close to what the customer was seeking, time and playing might make the difference. Some woods, such as spruce, have a reputation for opening up after a few weeks or months of playing, and many instruments continue to improve over the course of years. Acoustic research has encouraged speculation that this maturing process is a result of changes to the wood at the cellular level that are caused by vibration and aging. Most luthiers have a good idea of how much change to expect in the sound of their guitars, and some will allow you to trade the instrument in for another if you're unsatisfied with the tone after playing the instrument for a few weeks.

The care and feeding of a meticulously built custom instrument is the responsibility of the owner, so you must talk to the luthier about how best to care for your new guitar. Attention to humidity is paramount with acoustic instruments, and builders usually advise their customers to watch for extreme weather conditions, to monitor the humidity levels inside their guitar, and to use a guitar humidifier when necessary. Be sure to keep your instrument in a high-quality hard-shell case. The builder will set the guitar up for you before delivery and adjust the action to suit your preference, but you should also find out who to turn to down the road for expert adjustments to the neck, string action, electronics, etc. Many larger manufacturers will have assigned warranty stations, and some small builders also have authorized repair professionals you must go to lest you invalidate the warranty.

One additional item to keep in mind when choosing a luthier is that guitars built by the more established and respected builders, although often higher priced, will maintain their value and increase in value over the years if the instrument is well cared for. On the other hand, a luthier who has not been in business as long may do tremendous work and offer good prices while building his or her reputation.

CUSTOM SHOPS

One option is to order an instrument from the custom shop of a larger manufacturer, such as Gibson, Martin, or Guild. In most cases, you'll have to place your order through a retail store and work with one of the shop employees to examine standard models to determine which custom options you want. You can point to a specific model on the wall, for example, and say, "Order me a guitar just like this but with koa back and sides, a Sitka spruce top, and my name emblazoned in abalone at the 12th fret."

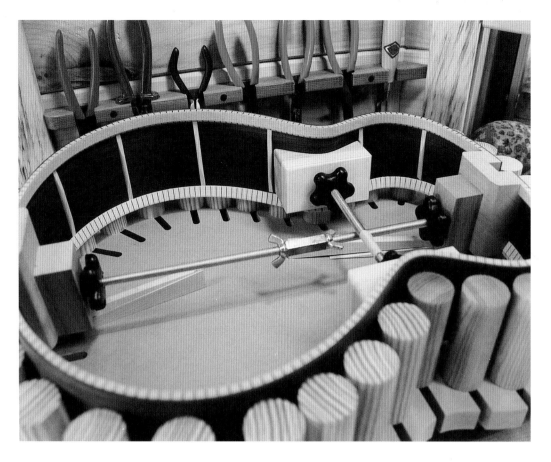

dozen employees who help him build 12 different models, and 50 percent of the company's orders are for custom guitars. The guitars are ordered through a dealer, but Santa Cruz expects to spend some time on the phone with the customer early in the process. "My preference is to talk directly to the player," says Hoover. "It's better to get the information from the customer about what they want." Santa Cruz offers a limited lifetime warranty to the original owner and supplies a list of approved repair shops around the country who are authorized to handle warranty work.

Michael Millard of Froggy Bottom Guitars has been building guitars since 1969. His company currently builds 100–125 guitars per year and sells about 35 percent of them direct to customers and the other 65 percent through dealers. The basic Froggy Bottom production flattop features mahogany back and sides, a Sitka spruce top, and curly maple binding. There are 15 basic body styles to choose from as well as an incredible variety of options. "We go to truly great lengths to make the right guitar for the player," says Millard. "We work with a dozen or more different woods, a variety of plate thicknesses, and a broad array of scale lengths. We build 12-strings, parlors, and baritone guitars as well."

Some custom shops, such as Guild's in Nashville, deal directly with customers as well as working through a local dealer. Guild's production manager, Mark Kendrick, notes that players tend to be more traditional when it comes to Guild instruments, but the shop still gets special requests on everything from inlay work to custom colors. His shop will supply almost any variety of woods or options the player requests, "as long as the instrument has structural integrity."

MIDSIZED SHOPS

The Santa Cruz Guitar Co., founded in 1977 by Richard Hoover, is an example of a midsized shop that has built a serious reputation for quality steel-string guitars. Santa Cruz guitars feature a lot of handwork, although more than 650 are currently produced each year. Hoover has a

Sides in progress in the True North Guitars shop.

INDIVIDUAL MAKERS

Many makers work independently and complete only a handful of instruments each year. One example is Don Musser, who builds fewer than a dozen classical guitars and flattop steel-strings per year in his shop in the Colorado Rockies. He offers four basic body shapes: a parlor, a classical, an orchestra model, and a dreadnought. Like many luthiers, Musser shies away from custom body shapes due to the effort that goes into creating molds. His guitars can be purchased direct or through specific shops and dealers (note that some individual makers *only* sell direct). He offers many custom options and selects the tonewoods to suit the player. "The number one question I ask my customers is what they hope to use the guitar for," he says, "in the studio, for personal enjoyment, or (God forbid) for touring. Based on what the person tells me, I tailor the woods to achieve their goals." Musser works most frequently with Indian and Brazilian rosewood for backs and sides, and he offers a variety of choices for soundboards. "I avoid cedar or redwood tops for people who are planning to use the guitar in the studio because those are overtone-rich and don't give as condensed a sound as some of the hard spruces like Sitka. Engelmann spruce is a balanced wood and can be colored one way or the other, depending on how the top is braced." Musser works out the details with his customers, gets a 20 percent deposit, and then sends a letter to the customer confirming the deal and the instrument's specifications.

SPECIALTY GUITARS

Canadian luthier Shelley Park has carved out a niche building replicas of Selmer and Maccaferri guitars, which are used to play the Gypsy jazz music popularized by Django Reinhardt in the 1920s and '30s. Park currently builds about 20 guitars per year in her Vancouver, B.C., shop. Before starting her own business, she worked as an apprentice for many years with Jean Larrivée and David Webber. Park, who spends her weekends gigging in Seattle with a Gypsy jazz band called Pearl Django, endeavors to help potential customers find instruments they can test before ordering, but it's difficult because her guitars are spread out over North America. "By and large," she says, "my guitars are bought sight unseen. It takes a lot of e-mail and phone calls. If the finished guitar was not what the customer expected, I would make it right or let the customer return the instrument. But so far, my customers have liked the instrument 100 percent of the time."

GUITAR BOUTIQUES

More and more guitar shops all over the country carry guitars by small and midsized builders in addition to larger manufacturers, and they place custom orders on a regular basis. Joe Caruso, who runs the Music Emporium in Lexington, Massachusetts, takes custom orders for Martins, midsized builders like Santa Cruz and Collings, and smaller builders such as James Goodall and Eric Schoenberg. "Some people want something fancy and unlike anything anyone else is going to have," Caruso says. "Sometimes they just want a Collings D-2H but with snowflake inlays instead of diamond-shaped inlays on the fretboard. The smaller builders offer many features and options, such as different neck widths, different spacing at the bridge, and different woods, and some players are willing to wait for those options."

At McCabe's Guitar Shop in Santa Monica, California, Nancy Felixson and Amilcar Dohrn-Melendez specialize in placing custom orders and act as go-betweens between the buyer and the builder. "If a customer has particular questions," Felixson says, "they can talk to the builder. One person wanted a particular grain of koa on a custom Goodall, so he talked directly to James Goodall." Many builders supply shops with brochures and lists of custom options, which customers can refer to. In ordering a custom Martin, McCabe's forwards the desired options to the Martin Custom Shop, and Martin then comes back with a price quote. Even when taking an order through a store, most builders are willing to work directly with the customer to help with decisions about woods and options. "Part of the experience of having a guitar made for you is to be as involved as possible in all of the aspects of the instrument's details," Dohrn-Melendez explains.

Kit Simon, who runs the Olde Town Pickin' Parlor in Arvada, Colorado, has been in business for many years and sees the future of his business closely intertwined with custom builders. He intends to focus on "boutique instruments" in the future, individually made guitars by a wide range of builders. "That's the direction I'm headed in," he says, "because I don't want to compete with the Guitar Centers. I want to be a prestigious store featuring custom guitars." Simon already works with such custom builders as Eric Schoenberg, Kevin Ryan, and Lance McCollum, and he keeps his eye out for up-and-coming builders. The ordering procedure varies depending on the preference of the builder. Collings allows Simon to handle most of the discussions with the customer, for example, while Lance McCollum encourages clients to call and discuss details and even visit him in his shop.

INSTRUMENT DEALERS

Some instrument dealers work from their homes rather than storefronts. They have working relationships with a number of builders and facilitate the ordering process for their clients for a moderate fee. The assistance of an experienced dealer can be very helpful, especially if you're ordering a guitar from another country. John Silva, formerly with classical dealer Guitar Salon International and now working independently with both nylon- and steel-string makers, has helped many customers order the guitars of their dreams. Ordering a classical guitar from Spain presents some unique challenges. "Trying to get a classical from a top Spanish builder would be much harder without the help of someone who is familiar with the builders," says Silva. "There are certain luthiers who won't change

anything in their design, and it helps to know the builders, their quirks, and what they're willing to do."

THE MAKER-PLAYER CONNECTION

Some musicians seek a distinctive sound, and they will go to great lengths to find what they are looking for. Fingerstyle jazz guitarist Woody Mann worked with California luthier Kevin Ryan to design a flattop steel-string with a particular response. He went to Ryan because he felt that Ryan's approach to building was similar in philosophy to that of late luthier James D'Aquisto. "Jimmy D'Aquisto was a great friend," Mann says, "and I played his archtop guitars for years. His guitars just sing. When I met Kevin, he had a similar, experimental attitude, and he said, 'Let's work together.'"

Nylon-string player Muriel Anderson started out playing bluegrass on Martin guitars. She studied classical guitar with Christopher Parkening and began playing a Hernandez classical and then went on to purchase a Ramírez (one of the great Spanish makers) when she could afford it. Eventually she picked up a used guitar built by Nashville luthier Paul McGill, and the McGill classical guitar has since become an integral part of Anderson's sound. Since she began touring with the guitar, McGill has had many requests from other players who ask him to build them a guitar like Anderson's. McGill and Anderson decided to collaborate on the design for a slightly higher-end model, the Model M, which has become quite popular. In the quest for a variety of tones and textures, Anderson has gone on to order a steel-string from Kevin Ryan and a harp guitar from Michigan builder Del Langejans.

Most everyone who orders a custom instrument finds the experience to be an exhilarating meeting of the minds between themselves and the builder. It's a creative adventure, and the result is a work of art uniquely matched to your music, technique, body, and spirit.

Understanding Tonewoods

Dana Bourgeois

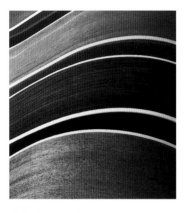

Why is it that different woods are used for acoustic guitars, and how do these woods affect the sound of the instrument? In the past, there was less opportunity for confusion on this issue, since most guitars were made of mahogany, rosewood, maple, ebony, and spruce. But with the dwindling availability of traditional tonewoods, particularly those cut from old-growth forests, major manufacturers and smaller luthiers alike have been compelled to consider the use of alternative species of tonewoods—some common and others more exotic. This chapter looks at the strengths and shortcomings of the woods most commonly used today for tops, backs and sides, fretboards, necks, and bridges.

EVALUATING TONEWOODS

Differences between woods can seem as mysterious and complex as differences between people. Even within a species, no two pieces of wood are exactly alike. Environmental conditions, genetics, the age of the tree, annular growth patterns, grain orientation, curing conditions, and so on all have an effect on the tonal properties of an individual piece of wood. In addition, tonewoods respond differently in the hands of different makers. They can also take on different characteristics when used in different models of guitars—even those built by the same maker. And whether a particular wood sounds good or bad depends upon who's doing the listening. So any attempt to sort out distinctions between tonewoods can only be offered from a subjective point of view.

When evaluating tonewoods, luthiers must take into account a wide variety of factors, some of which can be inscrutably subtle, and most of which are likely to vary in priority from one luthier to another. I tend to place a good deal of importance on a couple of elements that, when viewed together, illuminate much of my own understanding of tonewoods. *Velocity of sound* refers to the speed at which a material transmits received energy. Simply described, plucked guitar strings transmit energy to the bridge. The bridge in turn oscillates one surface of a ported enclosure, setting up sound pressure waves that eventually reach the eardrum. In order to control this chain reaction, one must design an efficient ported enclosure and then make it out of materials that facilitate the transmission of vibrational energy. Lively materials—those with a high velocity of sound, or low internal damping—make the best facilitators.

There are a number of ways in which luthiers judge the sound velocity of wood. The most common method is to hold the wood at a nodal point, tap it, and then listen for the response. This is analogous to playing the harmonic on a string. The difference between a high and a low velocity of sound can often be startlingly apparent. Sometimes a

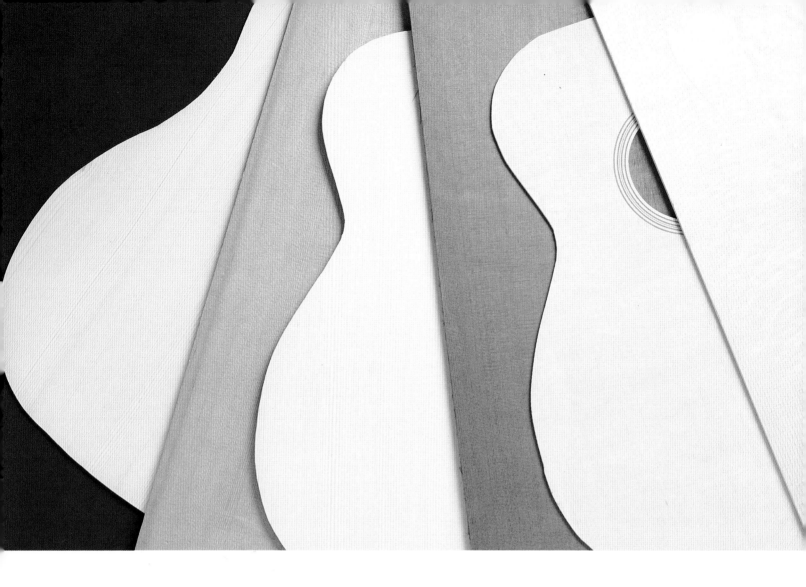

piece of wood is so lively that it doesn't matter where you tap it or where you hold it. I remember going through a large stack of aged Brazilian rosewood from which I was able to make my selection almost from the moment I lifted a piece off the top of the pile; rubbing one piece of wood against another was enough to make the best sets ring!

In addition to testing for velocity of sound, luthiers also make use of the tapping technique to listen for harmonic content. Like a string, a piece of wood is capable of producing a fundamental tone and an array of harmonics. Though the presence and strengths of individual harmonics are distinctly influenced by changes in the geometry and mass of the piece of wood, elements such as clarity of tone, relative harmonic complexity, and high, low, or mid

bias can readily be discovered by holding and tapping a piece of wood in a variety of ways.

TOPWOODS

Each part of the guitar seems to play a role, be it significant or subtle, in determining the tonal characteristics of the instrument. In very general terms, the top, or soundboard, seems to affect the guitar's responsiveness, the quickness of its attack, its sustain, some of its overtone coloration, and the strength and quality of each note's fundamental tone. Most luthiers, but not all, believe that the wood chosen for the top is the single overriding variable that determines the quality of tone of a finished instrument.

Some typical woods used to build soundboards (from left to right): eastern red spruce, western red cedar, European spruce, redwood, Sitka spruce with a faint bearclaw figure, and Engelmann spruce with a pronounced bearclaw figure (photo by David Etnier).

Spruce is the standard material for soundboards. These days the most commonly used species is Sitka, due to its availability and to the high yield from its characteristically large-diameter logs. Quartersawn Sitka is quite stiff along and across the grain; high stiffness, combined with the relatively light weight characteristic of most softwoods, is a recipe for high velocity of sound. A strong fundamental-to-overtone ratio gives Sitka a powerful, direct tone capable of retaining its clarity when played forcefully. Sitka is an excellent choice of topwood, then, for players whose style demands a wide dynamic response and a robust, meaty tone. On the other side of the balance sheet, the lack of a complex overtone component can result in a somewhat thinner tone when played with a light touch—depending, of course, upon the design of the guitar and the other woods used in its construction. The break-in period for a new Sitka guitar can also be longer than that of other spruces.

The most common alternative to Sitka is Engelmann spruce, another domestic western species. Engelmann is often more expensive than Sitka due to the lower yield from its smaller logs and because most logs have a spiral-grained structure that renders them unsuitable for proper quarter-sawing. Engelmann is considerably lighter in color than Sitka spruce, lighter in weight, and usually less stiff along the grain, resulting in a slightly lower velocity of sound. Engelmann also tends to exhibit a weaker fundamental tone, although it produces a noticeably broader and stronger overtone component. It is therefore a good choice for players who require a richer, more complex tone than can be obtained from most Sitka tops, particularly when the instrument is not played forcefully. The downside is that Engelmann guitars can have lower "headroom" than Sitka guitars, which is to say that clarity and definition are often sacrificed when an Engelmann guitar is played loudly.

European or silver spruce, the spruce of choice for makers of classical guitars, shares a number of characteristics with Engelmann spruce, including color, lightness of weight, harmonic complexity, and fullness at the lower end of the dynamic range. Because of its visual similarity and significantly higher cost, its name has been affixed more than once to a piece of Engelmann spruce by unscrupulous (or uninformed) wood dealers and luthiers. European spruce differs from Engelmann in its potentially quicker response and greater headroom, which results from its significantly greater stiffness, particularly along the grain. The availability of anything better than mediocre European spruce, which is often exceeded in quality by the better grades of Engelmann, is sharply limited, unless selected at the source in Europe.

Eastern red spruce, also known as Adirondack or Appalachian spruce, was the primary topwood used by American manufacturers before World War II. Its use was all but discontinued due to overharvesting of the resource but has recently been reintroduced thanks to 50 years of regeneration and to the legendary status that this traditional tonewood has attained. The small size of most logs and a shortage of wood conforming to market preference for even color and regularity of grain conspire to keep the price of red spruce extremely high.

Red spruce is relatively heavy, has a high velocity of sound, and has the highest stiffness across and along the grain of all the topwoods. Like Sitka, it has strong fundamentals, but it also exhibits a more complex overtone content. Tops made of red spruce have the highest volume ceiling of any species, yet they also have a rich fullness of tone that retains clarity at all dynamic levels. In short, red spruce may well be the Holy Grail of topwoods for the steel-string guitar. If players and builders are able to overcome phobias about unevenness of color, grain irregularity, minor knots, and four-piece tops, many more great-sounding guitars could be produced while the supply of potentially usable red spruce is still available. Old-growth woods are disappearing so quickly that an attitude change will need to be scheduled sometime in the near future, unless the majority of new guitars are to be made of synthetic materials.

Before leaving the spruces, I should mention bearclaw figure, or hazelfichte—a delightful pattern in the grain occasionally occurring in all species of spruce. Bearclaw, like the curl in curly maple, is a rippling of the longitudinal fibers that divides the surface of the wood into shimmering reflective patterns. Unlike the even waves that usually occur in maple, bearclaw usually appears in asymmetrical or randomly broken patterns. This phenomenon almost always occurs in older trees that have dense, stiff grain structure and correspondingly high sound velocity. Thus bearclaw is usually a reliable indicator of the more desirable attributes of spruce topwoods.

Western red cedar ranges in color from honey brown to light chocolate. It has a quickness of sound that exceeds any of the spruces, a higher overtone content, lower fundamental content, and lower stiffness along the grain. Since World War II, cedar has been used extensively by makers of classical guitars. Cedar-topped guitars are characteristically lush, dark-toned, and bursting with flavor. They are often less powerful in projection than their spruce cousins, however, and tend to lose clarity near the top of their dynamic range. Having enough bottom end is never a problem for a cedar guitar, although preventing the sound from getting muddy sometimes is.

Redwood is usually darker in color than cedar and often stiffer and heavier. Though lacking in cedar's overtone complexity, redwood's potentially stronger fundamental component makes it a good choice for someone interested in a cedarlike sound, but with greater definition and headroom. Old-growth redwood is perhaps the most protected of all domestic species, explaining why this potentially significant tonewood will probably never achieve the popularity it might otherwise enjoy.

Koa and mahogany have been used for soundboards since the '20s. More recently, some makers have begun to use a variety of other hardwoods for tops, such as walnut, maple, and even lacewood. When compared to soft woods, these hardwoods have in common a relatively low velocity of sound, considerable density, and a low overtone content. They therefore tend to produce a solid tone—though not an especially rich one—and respond best at the upper end of the dynamic range.

Mahogany-topped guitars exhibit a strong "punchy" tone that is well-suited to country blues playing. Koa has a somewhat more midrangey tone that works well for playing rhythm and truly shines in guitars made for Hawaiian-style slide playing. Because of its relatively similar sound velocity and weight characteristics, walnut has a "musical" tone within the range of mahogany and koa. On the other hand, maple, as a result of its greater weight and lower sound velocity, can be downright flat-sounding—a blessing in disguise when a guitar is amplified at high sound-pressure levels. This is also true of some of the more exotic species of hardwoods when used for tops.

Though not exactly classifiable as a species, plywood has probably seen as much use as solid woods for soundboard construction. Important factors influencing the quality of a plywood top are the number and thickness of the plies, the species of woods used, and the type of glue used. Most plywood used in guitar manufacturing has a low velocity of sound primarily as a result of the damping characteristics of lower-quality "filler" plies used in the cores. This is not always the case. I once saw some unbraced backs made of three plies of Indian rosewood that had weight, flexibility, and tap-tone characteristics that I would expect of solid Indian rosewood. This example suggests that properly designed plywood has the potential to produce far better guitars than what has generally been seen in the past.

Significant attention has already been trained on the design and making of totally synthetic materials. Most of these efforts have focused on the use of carbon graphite fiber, a material widely used in the manufacture of boats, aircraft, and bicycle frames. Carbon graphite fiber may be assembled in myriad patterns, directions, thicknesses, and layers, bonded together by a variety of resins. Tops and backs made of carbon graphite fiber typically exhibit a velocity of sound even greater than wood, often showing stronger overtones, particularly in the upper register. If more is better, however, then it should only be a matter of time before the use of wood is discontinued altogether. In truth, the greatest challenge to designers of synthetic materials may well be the players' expectations, which have taken several centuries to evolve to their present state.

BACKS AND SIDES

Besides serving to form the enclosure of the soundbox, the back and sides of the guitar also act as a sympathetic resonator whose oscillations contribute greatly to the harmonic mix. When judiciously selected, with due consideration given to design criteria and the other tonewoods used in the instrument, the back and sides can have a tremendous effect on the overall tone of the instrument. A sample of woods typically used to build backs and sides can be seen on page 120.

I categorize back and side materials into several distinct groupings: tonewoods that significantly color the sound of a guitar, relatively "transparent" tonewoods, and tonewoods that actually inhibit sound production through damping. These groupings will be used to illustrate the differences between commonly used back and side materials.

Rosewoods form a distinct subclassification within the group of tonewoods that contribute to tone coloration. Brazilian and Indian rosewoods are known for their high sound velocity and broad range of overtones. These actually unrelated woods, as well as their various rainforest cousins—cocobolo, kingwood, morado, and the like—are also characterized by strength and complexity in the bottom end and an overall darkness of tone in the rest of the range. Strong mids and highs also contribute a richness of tone to the upper registers. Equally important, guitars made of rosewood also have a pronounced "reverby" tone, caused by audible delays in the onset of certain harmonics.

I've found that Brazilian rosewood has everything that Indian rosewood has, only more—particularly in the top and bottom ends. Though both species exhibit complexity, darkness, and a reverby ring, Brazilian rosewood has tremendous clarity in the bottom end and sparkle in the top, while Indian rosewood has a thicker, more midrangey overall coloration.

The extreme scarcity of Brazilian rosewood, an internationally recognized endangered species, is well known to luthiers and players alike. An international embargo on trade in Brazilian rosewood products guarantees that the relatively few sets remaining in this country, which may be used only on domestically sold guitars, will continue to spiral in price as the supply dwindles. Issues regarding the availability of Indian rosewood, which is not an endangered species, are less widely understood. For years the Indian government has regulated the availability of logs from which nonfinished goods may be produced for export. In the past couple of years, increased enforcement efforts have resulted in a doubling of the price of Indian rosewood back and side sets. There has been additional debate within the Indian government about banning the export of Indian rosewood altogether in order to encourage investment in domestic manufacturing. India now has several guitar manufacturing facilities, and I am personally aware of several more in development. In my opinion it is only a matter of time before the emerging Indian guitar industry gains enough political clout to further restrict the export of Indian rosewood.

Mahogany and koa also have relatively high velocities of sound when considered as materials for backs and sides, and thus contribute much to overtone coloration. Lacking the low-end frequencies of the rosewoods and also their sustaining reverberation, these woods can have an altogether different sound. Where rosewood guitars may be thought of as having a "metallic" sound, mahogany and koa guitars are better described as sounding "woody"— although the harder, more dense examples of these woods

can also take on some of the characteristics of the rosewoods. Between the two, koa seems to have a little more fullness in the midrange, while mahogany tends to favor the bass and the treble.

Maple and walnut tend to be more acoustically transparent than other tonewoods, due to their lower velocity of sound and high degree of internal damping. That is to say, these woods tend to allow tonal characteristics of the top to be heard without the addition of significant coloration. The harder, denser examples of these woods, such as sugar maple and black walnut—particularly quartersawn exam-

ples—tend to lean slightly more in the tonal direction of mahogany, while softer examples, such as big-leaf maple and claro walnut, tend toward greater tonal transparency. Curly, quilted, and bird's-eye figures do not seem to have much effect on the tone of the wood, but they can be used, like bearclaw, as an indicator of other properties. Quilted figure, for example, occurs most often in softer species and is best displayed when the wood is flat-sawn—two characteristics that tend to produce higher damping properties.

In recent years a variety of new tonewoods have been introduced for use as back and sides, including ovangkol,

An array of woods for building backs and sides (from left to right): Brazilian rosewood, curly koa, curly mahogany, East Indian rosewood, curly maple, and curly claro walnut (photo by David Etnier).

imbuia, myrtlewood, padauk, zebrawood, blackwood, ebony, cherry, cocobolo, kingwood, and morado. Though I do not claim personal experience with all of these materials, certain generalizations may be made. As previously noted, cocobolo, kingwood, and morado are similar to rosewoods. Cocobolo and kingwood have qualities more similar to Brazilian rosewood; morado, or Honduran rosewood, has the fuller midrange associated with the sound of Indian rosewood. Though walnutlike in appearance, imbuia is also reported to perform within the range of the rosewood family. In my opinion, the most promising replacement for generic rosewood is padauk, a wood that is downright red when sawn but mellows to a reddish tan when finished. Padauk is a nonendangered African species that grows to sufficient size for quartersawing and sounds somewhere between Brazilian and Indian rosewood, leaning somewhat toward the Brazilian side.

Ovangkol has a rosewoodlike appearance but is a medium-density wood with a mahogany-like tonality. Cherry and zebrawood lean toward acoustic transparency. Myrtlewood is reportedly in the range of maple, but with a bigger bottom end. Woods that are too dense to float, such as certain ebonies and some examples of cocobolo and blackwood, have such high coefficients of internal damping that they can actually rob energy from the soundboard. Extremely fine guitars have been built from these woods, however, proving that careful selection and sensitive treatment can yield spectacular results.

NECKS, FRETBOARDS, AND BRIDGES

Players of electric guitars with bolt-on necks have long been hip to the fact that neck and fretboard materials can have a significant bearing on tone. Maple necks can impart a bright, poppy tone that can do much to reinforce the top end of a large-bodied guitar, while mahogany necks help push the overall palette into a warmer, more woody tonal range.

Fretboard materials also exert an influence on overall tone, although they probably act more as icing on the cake than as a layer of the cake itself. Brazilian rosewood fretboards and their denser rain forest counterparts add sparkle and ring, and Indian rosewood fretboards can help fatten up the midrange. Wenge, a dense, dark-colored African hardwood unrelated to the rosewoods, has tonal properties remarkably similar to those of Brazilian rosewood.

Ebony, the traditional fingerboard material found on violins, classical guitars, and high-end steel-strings, has the lowest velocity of sound of all the woods commonly used in lutherie and has definite damping characteristics. This may not prove to be much of a problem for large-bodied guitars made out of red spruce or Brazilian rosewood, but it may be something to consider when designing smaller guitars, particularly those using some of the less resonant woods for tops and backs.

Bridge materials, like fretboards, cannot make or break an instrument, but they serve to enhance or edit the tonal contributions of other materials found in the guitar. The woods discussed above—ebony, Brazilian rosewood, and Indian rosewood—contribute similar tonal qualities when they are used as bridge materials as when they are used for fretboards.

It is important to remember that wood species can be responsible only for certain aspects of the tone of any guitar. Equally important are the design of the guitar, the skill of the maker, and the quality of the individual pieces of wood from which the guitar is made. Species selection can, however, be a determining factor in the creation of a very special guitar or a guitar designed for a specific purpose.

Custom Guitar Makers

How to Use These Listings

The following listings contain information on more than 200 custom guitar builders, ranging from independent luthiers who produce only a handful of instruments per year to midsize builders who sell guitars direct and through dealers to large, corporate custom shops where well-loved brands are modified according to the customer's specifications. We gathered this information by sending surveys to as many guitar makers as we could track down in February 2000 and included those makers who either specified that they build custom guitars or who produce such a small number of instruments per year (fewer than 1,000) that they are classified as custom by default. For each maker listed, you'll find a brief biography, the year that the luthier or company began selling instruments, the approximate annual production, the types of guitars offered (steel-string flattops, nylon-strings, archtops, etc.), the maker's specialty, available custom options, and complete contact information, including Web site addresses. We've also included each one of these builders in our directory of manufacturers at www.acousticguitar.com, where you can link to the makers' Web sites and gather some additional, more time-sensitive information, such as the maker's current prices and turnaround time for completing orders. We will periodically update those listings so that potential custom guitar buyers can easily get a sense of which instruments they can afford to order and how long they'll have to wait for the results.

—Simone Solondz

A FULLER SOUND

Warren Fuller came to guitar building in 1998 after 31 years as a self-employed architect and general contractor. He was inspired to design guitars when he inspected a factory-model guitar. His designer brain soon began to dream of something different. Three months later, he finished his first instrument, and he has since joined the Guild of American Luthiers, the Northern California Association of Luthiers, and the Association of Stringed Instrument Artisans, which have exposed him to many high-quality guitars. His specialty is the jumbo steel-string, and he strives to build guitars with excellent balance, sustain, and projection.

First year of production: 1998
Approximate annual production: 12
Percent custom instruments: 100
Types of guitars built: Steel-string flattops
Guitar pictured: p. 44

A Fuller Sound
2224 Coloma St.
Oakland, CA 94602
Phone/fax: (510) 482-1996
www.afullersound.com

ALLEN GUITARS

Randy Allen is a self-taught luthier who began repairing instruments around 1979 and started building acoustic guitars in the early '80s. His shop is located in the Sierra foothills of California, where he builds resophonic guitars, mandolins, and several models of acoustic guitars, including dreadnoughts, OMs, small jumbos, and parlor guitars. His specialty is lap-style resophonics. Allen is also an importer and supplier of exotic tonewoods and luthier supplies, and he runs a custom fret-slotting service for guitar manufacturers and individual luthiers. He also supplies inlay materials and casts guitar and mandolin tailpieces. He is a member of several guilds, including SVLG, NCAL, GAL, and ASIA. His work has been featured in *Acoustic Musician* (February 1998) and *Guitarmaker* (No. 36) and exhibited at various music festivals, including the Healdsburg Guitar Festival ('96, '97, and '99) and the Acoustic Guitar Festival ('98).

First year of production: 1982
Approximate annual production: 8
Percent custom instruments: 0
Types of guitars built: Steel-string flattops, resonator guitars
Primary output: Lap-style resophonics
Guitar pictured: p. 92

Allen Guitars
PO Box 1883
Colfax, CA 95713-1883
Phone/fax: (530) 346-6590
www.allenguitar.com

AMERICAN ACOUSTECH

The builders of American Acoustech guitars, Tom Lockwood and Dave Stutzman, know guitars as few others do. Lockwood worked for more than a decade as plant manager for Guild Guitars, where he supervised the building of thousands of fine instruments, and he visited factories throughout the world to learn the techniques of other manufacturers. Since the late 1960s, Stutzman's family business, Stutzman's Guitar Center, has had a worldwide reputation for selling, repairing, and customizing the best new and vintage guitars. Lockwood and Stutzman analyzed both recent and vintage guitar designs before settling on their own, which focuses on performance and provides a mellow, clear, and balanced sound, with excellent power and sustain. They handcraft each American Acoustech guitar in their Rochester, New York, workshop, using carefully selected natural woods.

First year of production: 1993
Approximate annual production: 400–500
Percent custom instruments: 0
Primary output: Steel-string flattops
Custom options: Pickup systems, spruce or cedar tops

American Acoustech
4405 Ridge Rd. W.
Rochester, NY 14626
Phone: (716) 352-5014
Fax: (716) 352-8614
www.americanacoustech.com

AMERICAN ARCHTOP GUITARS

Dale Unger, the founder and president of American Archtop Guitars, was raised in Nazareth, Pennsylvania, home of C.F. Martin and Co. and some of the world's finest guitar craftspeople. He built his first guitar with the help of Martin's Dick Boak in 1977. He later met and learned from master archtop builder Robert Benedetto, who inspired him to start American Archtop Guitars. Unger offers both six- and seven-string models and builds guitars with solid or laminated tops and backs.

First year of production: 1995
Approximate annual production: 20–25
Percent custom instruments: 100
Types of guitars built: Archtops

American Archtop Guitars
RD #6, Box 6379B
Stroudsburg, PA 18360
Phone: (570) 992-4956
www.sunlink.net/~aarchtop/

ANDERSEN STRINGED INSTRUMENTS

Steve Andersen built his first guitar in 1973 and has earned his living solely as a guitar maker since 1978. He specializes in custom-building to meet players' specific needs. Working alone, he builds two to four instruments at a time, generally completing 24 per year. His instruments have been sold across the U.S., as well as in more than a dozen countries around the world. His interest in archtops began in the early 1980s when he began listening to swing and jazz music. He built a few archtops but didn't get serious until he moved to Seattle, Washington, in 1986. He has had the opportunity to work on some of the best archtops of the 20th century and found it a powerful learning experience. While he's gone on to develop his own look and sound, he has definitely been influenced by the work of builders who came before him. In addition, he's found that his experience as a mandolin builder was valuable in understanding archtop guitars. Since 1990, most of his focus as a builder and most of his energy regarding innovations and new models has been on the archtop guitar.

First year of production: 1978
Approximate annual production: 24
Percent custom instruments: 85
Types of guitars built: Steel-string flattops, archtops
Primary output: Archtops
Guitar pictured: p. 80

Andersen Stringed Instruments
7811 Greenwood Ave. N.
Seattle, WA 98103
Phone: (206) 782-8630
Fax: (206) 782-9345
www.andersenguitars.com

ANGUS GUITARS

After building his first six guitars on his own, Mark Angus went to work for Bob Mattingly in the mid-'70s and learned repair, restoration, and guitar construction. He has been with the Guitar Shoppe in Laguna Beach, California, since 1990. In the early '80s, Carl Verheyen started playing his guitars, which resulted in the Carl Verheyen Studio model.

First year of production: 1976
Approximate annual production: 12
Percent custom instruments: 100
Types of guitars built: Steel-string flattops, nylon-strings
Primary output: Steel-string flattops
Custom options: Maple-bound headstock and bridge, inlay, abalone tops, cutaways
Guitar pictured: p. 14

Angus Guitars
PO Box 737
Laguna Beach, CA 92652-0737
Phone: (949) 497-3198
www.angusguitars.com

ANTIQUE ACOUSTICS

Rudolph Blazer started building guitars in the traditional German way, serving as an apprentice for an older guitar company in 1971. After working as a repairman for some time, he opened his own workshop in Stuttgart, in southern Germany. He then moved to his current hometown of Tübingen, where he started making steel-string guitars and mandolins with Wilhelm Henkes. The two also specialized in repairing and restoring prewar American guitars and began to re-create many of the old models, such as dreadnoughts, OMs, 12-fret steel-strings, jumbos, and ladder-braced 12-strings, using old-fashioned techniques and original materials. They build a wide range of prewar re-creations and offer traditional and custom pearl inlays.

Approximate annual production: 30
Percent custom instruments: 66
Types of guitars built: Steel-string flattops, 12-strings, archtops
Primary output: steel-string flattops
Custom options: Custom neck sizes, pearl inlays

Antique Acoustics
Jakobsgasse 14
72070 Tübingen
Germany
Phone: (49) 7071-550958
Fax: (49) 7071-550958

ROB ARMSTRONG

Rob Armstrong has been a professional musical instrument maker since 1971. His personal philosophy is to seek to understand what makes a fine instrument, both by considering the established traditions and by experimental work. He specializes in acoustic instruments—six- and 12-string guitars, mandolins, mandocellos, basses, parlor guitars, and other custom instruments. Each instrument is handmade from seasoned tonewoods—including spruce, cedar, pine, mahogany, rosewood, maple, walnut, and ebony. Armstrong works alone using basic hand tools and is thus wholly responsible for the quality of each instrument. His often unorthodox and inquiring approach has produced a wide variety of custom instruments, including long-scale guitars, baby guitars, "humbuckoustics," and double-necks. His instruments are played by such musicians as Gordon Giltrap, Bert Jansch, and George Harrison.

First year of production: 1971
Approximate annual production: 12–15
Percent custom instruments: 100
Types of guitars built: Steel-string flattops, 12-strings, nylon-strings, specialty guitars
Primary output: Steel-string flattops

Rob Armstrong
52 Stratford St.
Coventry CV2 4NJ, England
Phone: (44) 24-7644-2502

ATKIN GUITARS

Alister Atkin built his first guitar at school and went on to study guitar making at the London School of Furniture. There he learned to make classical guitars under the direction of top luthier David Whiteman. After graduating, he worked with a Canterbury-based guitar builder/repairer (Andy Crockett) and pursued his real interest: steel-string acoustic guitars. When his workload started to grow, he set up Atkin Guitars and moved into his own workshop in the village of Bridge, near Canterbury. As Atkin Guitars has grown, Atkin has invested in more sophisticated tools and continued developing his skills and techniques to build ever finer instruments. Drawing inspiration from both British and U.S. guitar makers, he has been able to find his own place in a growing market, and his guitars are now sold in several European countries.

First year of production: 1993
Approximate annual production: 40
Percent custom instruments: 25
Types of guitars built: Steel-string flattops, 12-strings, specialty guitars
Primary output: Steel-string flattops
Guitar pictured: p. 39

Atkin Guitars
19 Riverside Close
Bridge Canterbury
Kent CT4 5BN, England
Phone: (44) 1227-830050
www.atkinguitars.com

JAMES R. BAKER GUITARS

In 1960 James R. Baker signed up for guitar lessons with an elderly man who taught in his neighborhood and played a Selmer guitar. Baker's first guitar was a Silvertone archtop, which he fell in love with. His family goes back generations as woodworkers, and Baker himself is a master woodworker and skilled machinist who spent many years working for design firms. He began building guitars in 1971 (copying Strats and Martins) and began working on the design for his archtop guitars in 1994, speaking to players about their needs and carefully developing the technical and visual aspects of his striking, lightweight archtop guitars.

First year of production: 1996
Approximate annual production: 15–20
Percent custom instruments: 100
Types of guitars built: Steel-string flattops, 12-strings, nylon-strings
Primary output: Archtops

James R. Baker Guitars
PO Box 398
Shoreham, NY 11786
Phone: (631) 821-6935
www.li.net/~jbaker

BARANIK GUITARS

Mike Baranik's interest in guitar making began when he saw an ad in a music magazine for the Roberto-Venn School of Luthiery in Phoenix, Arizona. He attended the school's fall class of 1993 and was immediately hooked on the craft. Upon graduating he went on to serve as an assistant instructor, which allowed him to take part in a very productive learning environment while developing his own guitar-making skills. Baranik joined the Phoenix Guitar Co. in 1994, where he specialized in building custom acoustic and electric guitars and repairing vintage instruments. With his expanding inventory of exotic woods and tools, Baranik decided to set up his own shop in 1995. Baranik strives for a simple, elegant style, where the beauty of the wood is the main focus. Each guitar top is individually voiced for balanced tone and volume, and different types of woods are used to maximize the guitar's overall sound. Each guitar is set up for comfortable play with immaculate fretwork and an intonated saddle. A choice of different scale lengths and optional nut/string spacing is available to match the player's specific needs.

First year of production: 1995
Approximate annual production: 20–24
Percent custom instruments: 75
Types of guitars built: Steel-string flattops
Custom options: Woods, scale length, string spacing, body depth
Guitar pictured: p. 15

Baranik Guitars
1739 E. Broadway Rd.
Tempe, AZ 85282

Phone: (480) 755-3823
www.baranikguitars.com

BEAR CREEK GUITARS

Bill Hardin has been building guitars since the early '80s, working for OMI Dobro and the Santa Cruz Guitar Co. before starting his own company, Bear Creek Guitars, in 1995. His love of Hawaiian guitars started at Dobro, where he met Don Young (now the owner of National Reso-Phonic Guitars), whose enthusiasm for Hawaiian music and steel guitars inspired Hardin's interest in these exotic instruments. Hardin currently builds Hawaiian steel guitars in the Weissenborn tradition. They are styled after the classic steel guitars of the 1920s but feature beautiful craftsmanship and much more attention to detail than the originals. He handcrafts each of his instruments, using the finest highly figured Hawaiian koa available today. He also builds rope-bound ukuleles with highly figured or plain koa in soprano, concert, tenor, and baritone sizes. His guitars are played by Bob Brozman, one of the world's greatest traditional steel players.

First year of production: 1995
Approximate annual production: 12
Percent custom instruments: 100
Types of guitars built: Hawaiian guitars
Guitar pictured: p. 95

Bear Creek Guitars
PO Box 1057
Volcano, HI 96785
Phone: (808) 985-7555
Fax: (808) 985-7565
www.bcguitar.com

BELTONA

Beltona is a small, specialist enterprise relying on the complementary and individual skills of luthier Steve Evans and engineer Bill Johnson. Beltona was formed in the U.K. in 1991 with the aim of producing the finest metal-bodied instruments possible. It now has a worldwide reputation and market and ensures the highest quality by designing and producing all components of every instrument. Johnson's wide-ranging curiosity and expertise in metalworking led him to discover metal resonator instruments. Evans had many years of experience in guitar making, repair, and restoration in his native New Zealand and in the U.K. Together they set out to improve the distinctive tones of the resonator guitar, beginning with their favorite (and the most complex): the triple resonator. Following the success of this instrument, other models were developed. Beltona is now based in New Zealand and continues to serve its worldwide market with a range of standard instruments and one-off creations. Each instrument is individually hand-

crafted and made to order, allowing for individual specifications and requirements.

First year of production: 1991
Approximate annual production: 30
Percent custom instruments: 50
Types of guitars built: Resonator guitars
Primary output: Metal-bodied resophonic guitars
Custom options: Cutaways, engravings, inlays
Guitar pictured: p. 88

Beltona
Old Parua Bay Rd.
R. D. 5 Whansare 1
New Zealand
Phone: (64) 9-438-3313
Fax: (64) 9-438-3361

ROBERT BENEDETTO

Noted archtop guitar maker Robert Benedetto has been building guitars since 1968 and violins since 1983. During his prolific career, he has handcrafted more than 750 musical instruments (including 450 archtops), which are played by such noted artists as Bucky Pizzarelli, Kenny Burrell, Jimmy Bruno, Howard Alden, Jack Wilkins, Martin Taylor, Stéphane Grappelli, Andy Summers, and Earl Klugh. His highly sought-after instruments have price tags of up to $100,000. Benedetto has attained an unrivaled depth of understanding of the archtop guitar, bringing the instrument to an unprecedented degree of refinement. Profiled extensively in books and magazines, his guitars appear on countless recordings, videos, TV shows, film and television soundtracks, and at concerts, museums, and jazz festivals worldwide. In 1994 Benedetto authored the landmark book *Making an Archtop Guitar* and followed that with his 1996 video *Archtop Guitar Design and Construction*. In March 1999, he signed a licensing agreement with Fender/Guild to have Benedetto models made at Guild's Custom shop in Nashville.

First year of production: 1968
Approximate annual production: 20–25
Percent custom instruments: 100
Types of guitars built: Archtops
Custom options: Body size, neck dimensions, woods, inlays, bindings
Guitar pictured: p. 78

Robert Benedetto
830 Resica Falls Rd.
E. Stroudsburg, PA 18301-9741
Phone: (570) 223-0883
Fax: (570) 223-7711
www.benedetto-guitars.com

BEYOND THE TREES

Fred Carlson of Beyond the Trees Original and Custom Stringed Instruments built his first musical instrument in 1972 as part of an alter-

native high school program in rural Vermont. He spent the next several years working as an informal apprentice, exploring the world where music and sculpture meet. He later attended the Center for Guitar Research and Design, where he learned the basics of guitar building from luthier/teacher extraordinaire Charles Fox. In the years since, he has been blessed with opportunities to learn about and create a wide variety of musical instruments, including guitars, dulcimers, wooden banjos, early bowed instruments, thumb pianos, and flutes. He continues to develop the Sympitar, his unique acoustic guitar with added sympathetic strings, and several guitarists are now performing and recording with this instrument. Carlson lives and works with his partner, violin builder and herbalist Suzy Norris, in the coastal hills near Santa Cruz, California.

First year of production: 1976
Approximate annual production: 3–10
Percent custom instruments: 90
Types of guitars built: Steel-string flattops, 12-strings, nylon-strings, archtops, Hawaiian guitars, specialty guitars
Primary output: Specialty guitars
Guitar pictured: p. 101

Beyond the Trees
1987 Smith Grade
Santa Cruz, CA 95060
Phone: (408) 423-9264
www.beyondthetrees.com

BISCHOFF GUITARS

After studying performance on saxophone and guitar at the University of Wisconsin, Gordon Bischoff attended Redwing Technical College in Redwing, Minnesota, where he learned the art of violin repair. He used the skills and techniques from that training, as well as everything he could learn from available printed material, to pursue his true interest: building guitars. His career is made up of designing and developing handmade guitars, repairing guitars, and 15 years as a professional musician. He believes that the combination of these three disciplines has helped make him a better luthier. His annual production is small, allowing him to give the customer a rare opportunity to have input in the making of the instrument. For Bischoff, this collaboration can be as satisfying as building the guitar itself.

First year of production: 1975
Approximate annual production: 6
Percent custom instruments: 100
Types of guitars built: Steel-string flattops, 12-strings
Primary output: Steel-strings
Guitars pictured: pp. 30, 55

Bischoff Guitars
5150 Deerfield Rd.

Eau Claire, WI 54701-8713
Phone: (715) 834-3751
www.bischoffguitars.com

BISHLINE GUITARS

Robert Bishline graduated from the Roberto-Venn School of Luthiery in Phoenix, Arizona, in 1983. There he studied with John Roberts and William Eaton. He started repairing instruments at the Guitar House of Tulsa in 1984, where he is still employed. His repair work has allowed him to closely study all types of acoustic guitars. He builds custom guitars by special order and for his own experimentation, building just a few guitars a year, along with special instruments such as archtop mandolins, banjos, and resonator guitars.

First year of production: 1985
Approximate annual production: 5
Percent custom instruments: 100
Types of guitars built: Steel-string flattops, resonator guitars
Primary output: Steel-string flattops
Custom options: Woods, inlays
Guitar pictured: p. 32

Bishline Guitars
1730 S. 140th E. Ave.
Tulsa, OK 74108
Phone: (918) 835-6959

TOM BLACKSHEAR

Tom Blackshear played flamenco guitar professionally for about 17 years and built his first guitar in 1958. Guitar building was a secondary business for him until 1974, when his enthusiasm for the craft reached a crescendo. His career has been focused on building classical guitars ever since.

First year of production: 1958
Approximate annual production: 12–25
Percent custom instruments: 0
Types of guitars built: Nylon-strings
Primary output: Classicals and flamencos
Guitar pictured: p. 59

Tom Blackshear
17303 Springhill Dr.
San Antonio, TX 78232-1552
Phone/fax: (210) 494-1141
http://tguitars.home.texas.net/
    index.htm

BLANCHARD GUITARS

Mark Blanchard started repairing and restoring stringed instruments in 1981 while he was working on his degree at the University of California at Santa Cruz. He has an extensive background in physics, metal machining, and fine woodworking and finds lutherie to be the perfect blend of science, precision handcraft, and art. In 1994 he introduced his own line of custom steel- and nylon-string acoustic guitars. Although he is largely self-taught, Blanchard had the great fortune of studying scientific acoustic theory under Al Carruth in 1996. Carruth's methods of free plate tuning allow precise control over the voicing process and have helped Blanchard consistently produce high-quality guitars. In 1998, after 17 years of part-time lutherie, Blanchard became a full-time builder. Blanchard loves working closely with each patron to design the perfect custom instrument. This interaction is an important part of the building process, and the friendships he has developed with his patrons around the world have been the highlight of his career.

First year of production: 1994
Approximate annual production: 12–16
Percent custom instruments: 100
Types of guitars built: Steel-string flattops, 12-strings, nylon-strings
Custom options: Various woods, cutaways, purfling, scale lengths, inlays
Guitar pictured: p. 42

Blanchard Guitars
PO Box 8030
Mammoth Lakes, CA 93546
Phone: (760) 935-4351
www.blanchardguitars.com

BOAZ GUITARS

Boaz Elkayam was born in Israel in 1964 into a family of stringed-instrument builders. Although he builds eight concert-quality instruments per year, Boaz has always believed that the traditional guitar is acoustically flawed. He has spent half his life traveling the globe, searching for adventure and exchanging instrument-building knowledge with master builders. His wealth of information comes from talking with world-renowned musicians as well as indigenous people in South America about woods and carving techniques. He worked with brilliant physicist and acoustical engineer Dr. Michael Kasha and late luthier Richard Schneider, and he acts as a consultant, in conjunction with Kasha, to the Acoustical Physics Research Laboratory of the University of Florida at Tallahassee. Schneider once called Elkayam "the only luthier equipped to carry on my legacy. He knows my meaning, he understands what I'm after, and he's not afraid to try new things to improve the instrument, which is what I've dedicated my life to—perfecting the sound of the classical guitar."

First year of production: 1985
Approximate annual production: 6–8
Percent custom instruments: 100
Types of guitars built: Steel-string flattops, 12-strings, nylon-strings, archtops, specialty guitars
Primary output: Classicals
Custom options: Custom bracing, composite frets, Buzz Feiten intonation
Guitar pictured: p. 69

Boaz Guitars
9522 Topanga Canyon Blvd.
Chatsworth, CA 91311
Phone: (818) 772-8464
www.boazguitars.com

DANA BOURGEOIS

Dana Bourgeois is a well-known maker of traditionally styled bluegrass, fingerstyle, bottleneck, and archtop guitars. Over the years his instruments have been used by such diverse artists as Ricky Skaggs, Martin Simpson, Bryan Sutton, Ry Cooder, Henry Kaiser, Russ Barenberg, Vince Gill, David Lindley, Lee Roy Parnell, Marshall Crenshaw, Jerry Douglas, Elliott Easton, James Taylor, Ron Block and Dan Tyminski of Union Station, Andy York, James Pennebaker, Stephen Bruton, Ed Gerhard, and Guy Clark. A leading authority on tone production, Bourgeois has written articles on voicing, tonewood selection, and a variety of guitar-making subjects that have enjoyed wide circulation among builders and guitarists alike. He has worked with Martin, Schoenberg, Gibson, and Paul Reed Smith and is best known as founder of Dana Bourgeois Guitars. He currently builds custom handmade guitars in his shop in Lewiston, Maine.

First year of production: 1974
Approximate annual production: 30
Percent custom instruments: 100
Types of guitars built: Steel-string flattops, archtops
Custom options: A variety of woods, decorative appointments, finishes, hardware, and body and neck styles

Dana Bourgeois
2 Cedar St.
Lewiston, ME 04240
Phone: (207) 786-0385
www.bourgeoisguitars.com

BOWN GUITARS

Ralph Bown made his first guitar (a classical) while at school and has been building professionally since leaving university in 1979. He is essentially self-taught, although he received invaluable help and encouragement early on from established U.K. luthiers such as Paul Fischer, David Rubio, and Steve Phillips as well as numerous players. He began as a builder of classical guitars and still builds the odd nylon-string, but his emphasis shifted early on to steel-string flattop instruments, especially vintage American–style guitars, such as OMs, 00s, and 000s. These smaller-bodied instruments still account for a large part of his production. Bown has extended his love for traditional guitars to include Stella 12-string replicas, Maccaferri-style guitars, and instruments inspired by the designs of the Larson Brothers (Prairie State guitars and Dyer-style harp guitars). He is especially interested in developing harp guitar design. Alongside the more traditional designs, he has always enjoyed the challenge and variety of working with players to produce unusual and original instruments, such as his baritone and long-scale D guitars built in collaboration with Martin Simpson. He has also built instruments for Tom Chapin, Henry Kaiser, Kristina Olsen, John Renbourn, and Peter Rowan.

First year of production: 1981
Approximate annual production: 25–30
Percent custom instruments: 100
Types of guitars built: Steel-string flattops, 12-strings, specialty guitars
Primary output: Steel-string flattops
Custom options: Neck width and profile, design, woods, inlays
Guitars pictured: pp. 24, 103

Bown Guitars
1 Paver Lane, Walmgate
York Y01 9TS
England
Phone: (44) 1904-621001
www.ee.ed.ac.uk/~afm/music/bown/ralph.html

BOZO GUITARS

Bozo Podunavac is a Serbian-born luthier who emigrated to the U.S. in 1959. He served his apprenticeship with master Yugoslavian luthier Milutin Mladenovic before moving to Chicago, where he worked in the repair department of a musical instruments dealer and manufacturer. In 1964 he opened his own shop and began building Bozo guitars. He is best known for building guitars for Leo Kottke back in the early '70s. Whether plain or fancy, his guitars have a very distinctive voice and tone. They are particularly well balanced and have a commanding presence. Podunavac left the Chicago area in the mid-'70s and moved to southern California, where he opened a shop and school of lutherie in San Diego. He licensed several of his designs to a Japanese firm that proceeded to build several hundred Bozo guitars, some with laminated backs and sides, some with all solid wood construction. He had some health problems and stopped hand-crafting instruments for two decades but is now building guitars again. He has now completed more than 500 unique instruments.

First year of production: 1964
Approximate annual production: 6–8
Percent custom instruments: 100
Types of guitars built: Steel-string flattops, 12-strings, nylon-strings,
Primary output: Steel-string flattops
Custom options: Abalone and herringbone upgrades, all-wood bindings
Guitar pictured: p. 16

Bozo Guitars
2340 Englewood Rd.
Englewood, FL 34223

Phone: (941) 474-3288
Fax: (941) 473-8221

BREEDLOVE GUITAR CO.

When he moved to Tumalo, Oregon, to establish the Breedlove Guitar Co., Steve Henderson had a simple ambition: to build the finest guitars in the country. Ten years later, Breedlove has built a reputation for producing acoustic guitars and mandolins that are uncompromising in workmanship, extraordinary in sound, and among the most innovative in the industry in design and materials. Henderson has led the way in the use of indigenous American woods such as walnut and myrtlewood, and Breedlove offers perhaps the widest selection of tonewoods available from any luthier. Imaginative styling and design features such as a patented internal truss system produce instruments that are as distinctive in their appearance as in their rich bass response, brilliant treble, and remarkable playability. In the future, Henderson plans to introduce a line of nylon-string guitars and to continue growing and innovating while never losing the focus on quality.

First year of production: 1990
Approximate annual production: 600
Percent custom instruments: 75
Types of guitars built: Steel-string flattops, 12-strings, nylon-strings, specialty guitars
Custom options: Body depth, cutaways, neck width, woods, binding, inlays, body shapes
Guitar pictured: p. 45

Breedlove Guitar Co.
19885 Eighth St.
Tumalo, OR 97701-9042
Phone: (541) 385-8339
Fax: (541) 385-8183
www.breedloveguitars.com

FLETCHER BROCK STRINGED INSTRUMENTS

Fletcher Brock specializes in building archtop and flattop guitars, citterns, bouzoukis, and other mandolin-family instruments. He enjoys designing and building one-off or specialty projects. Occasionally these projects are so successful (the short-scale cittern, for example), that they become part of his permanent line. Brock is originally from Cape Cod, Massachusetts, where he grew up in an artistic and musical environment. In 1972 he moved to Providence, Rhode Island, and began assisting in vintage restoration and cutting mother-of-pearl and abalone inlay patterns for luthier Michael Allison's ornate banjos. It was this hands-on exposure to the instruments of yesteryear and the styles of music played on them that inspired Brock's career as a luthier and a performer. He built and sold his first mandolin in 1972 and relocated to the West Coast in 1979. His experience as a musician gives him a keen insight into sound, playability, and durability, and his instruments reflect 25 years of on-stage field testing. He builds instruments singularly or in small batches, designing, constructing, and finishing each instrument himself.

First year of production: 1992
Approximate annual production: 12
Percent custom instruments: 100
Types of guitars built: Steel-string flattops, 12-strings, archtops, specialty guitars
Guitar pictured: p. 72

Fletcher Brock Stringed Instruments
PO Box 5781
Ketchum, ID 83340
Phone: (208) 788-5439

BROOK GUITARS

After spending a number of years working with Andy Manson, one of England's most respected luthiers, Simon Smidmore and Andy Petherick formed Brook Guitars. The business was initially formed to produce A.B. Manson and Co.'s standard range of 20 instruments, including mandolins, bouzoukis, and multineck guitars, under a licensing arrangement that would allow Manson to concentrate on producing one-off instruments. In the meantime, however, Brook has expanded, and the company now employs a staff of three and offers a range of high-quality, handmade acoustic guitars under the Brook name. The workshop is located on the edge of Dartmoor in the southwest of England, a rural area that has become a center for musical instrument makers of all disciplines. This has created a pool of skills, knowledge, and facilities and provides a healthy interaction between makers. All Brook guitars are named after west country rivers and are built of locally cut timbers, such as flamed sycamore, cherry, walnut, lacewood, and yew, as well as the more traditional redwoods and mahoganies.

First year of production: 1993
Approximate annual production: 120
Percent custom instruments: 50
Types of guitars built: Steel-string flattops, 12-strings, nylon-strings, archtops, specialty guitars
Primary output: Steel-string flattops

Brook Guitars
Easterbrook, Hittisleigh
Exeter, Devon
EX6 6LR, England
Phone: (44) 1647-24139
Fax: (44) 1647-24140

S.B. BROWN GUITARS

Steve Brown began repairing guitars in 1965. In 1994 he began building OM-size guitars on a custom basis, and he now manufactures 24 guitars per year, all on commission. He is also heading up a project in Ethiopia that teaches young luthiers the art of guitar building.

First year of production: 1994
Approximate annual production: 24
Percent custom instruments: 100
Types of guitars built: Steel-string flattops
Custom options: Inlays, size, design

S.B. Brown Guitars
138 Marion Blvd.
Fullerton, CA 92835
Phone: (714) 526-1211

R.E. BRUNÉ

Richard Bruné began his career as a professional flamenco guitarist. Unable to afford a good guitar, he began making his own and was entirely self-taught. In order to better understand the instruments, he began collecting guitars, which became his de facto teachers. By 1973, when he moved to his present shop in Evanston, Illinois, he had too many orders to continue his playing career. Clients have included Andrés Segovia, the Romeros, Earl Klugh, Igor Kipnis, Julian Bream, Sabicas, El Moraito de Jerez, and many other notable artists.

First year of production: 1966
Approximate annual production: 20–25
Percent custom instruments: 100
Types of guitars built: Nylon-strings, specialty guitars
Primary output: Classicals and flamencos
Custom options: Scale, woods, neck sizes, string spacing, action, fret size, decoration
Guitars pictured: pp. 98, 104

R.E. Bruné
800 Greenwood St.
Evanston, IL 60201
Phone: (847) 864-7730
Fax: (847) 864-8022
www.rebrune.com

BURTON GUITARS

Cynthia H. Burton resides and works in Portland, Oregon, with her partner in life and lutherie, Jeff Elliott. In 1978 while working as an editor, she decided to take a guitar-making class to have a better instrument to play. The class took her to North Adams, Massachusetts, for an intensive six weeks with William Cumpiano. After an extremely positive experience, she decided it was time for a career change. After spending some more time in Cumpiano's shop and building a few more guitars, she headed for Oregon and the shop of then acquaintance Jeff Elliott. She started making classical guitars independently and occasionally collaborated with Elliott. In recent years she has devoted more and more time to the fine art of French-polishing—refinishing and repairing the finish on many modern and older guitars. She is a contributing editor to the Guild of American Luthiers' journal *American Lutherie*, is an officer and board member of the Portland Guitar Society, and helps organize Portland's annual Handmade Musical Instrument Exhibition.

First year of production: 1980
Approximate annual production: 4
Percent custom instruments: 100
Types of guitars built: Nylon-strings
Primary output: Classicals
Custom options: Rosettes, neck shapes, body shapes, cutaways

Burton Guitars
2812 S.E. 37th Ave.
Portland, OR 97202
Phone: (503) 233-0836

BUSCARINO GUITARS

John Buscarino is a luthier dedicated to the archtop guitar. He apprenticed with two master luthiers: Augustino LoPrinzi, from whom he learned the finer points of building classical guitars, and famed archtop builder Robert Benedetto, who says that Buscarino's instruments "rival those of the old masters and will certainly be prized by future generations." Buscarino believes that consistency is the ultimate test of a guitar's worth. He handcrafts each of his instruments to suit the customer's personal needs in his state-of-the-art workshop nestled in the western mountains of North Carolina. There he has created hundreds of exquisite guitars using proven methods passed down over generations. He is constantly refining these time-tested techniques, taking each instrument to a new level. Guitarist Steve Morse considers his Buscarino guitars "treasured works of art" as do many of Buscarino's customers.

First year of production: 1981
Approximate annual production: 50
Percent custom instruments: 100
Types of guitars built: Steel-string flattops, nylon-strings, archtops
Primary output: Archtops
Custom options: Block or vine inlays, snakewood accessories
Guitars pictured: pp. 64, 87

Buscarino Guitars
2348 Wide Horizon Dr.
Franklin, NC 28734
Phone: (828) 349-9867
Fax: (828) 349-4668
www.buscarino.com

GREGORY BYERS

Gregory Byers built his first guitar in around 1980 while finishing research for a Ph.D. in biology. He has never looked back. His two biggest influences in the early years were John Gilbert and José Romanillos, with whom he attended two workshops. He has also learned by examining the guitars of many fine luthiers. Byers devised and published a scientifically inspired system of intonation for the classical guitar, which he applies to all his instruments. His current research interest is in the realm of optimal soundboard design. Although most of the instruments he builds are classical guitars, he has a great affection for flamenco music and occasionally makes traditional flamenco guitars. His instruments are played and recorded by many fine artists, including David Russell, David Tanenbaum, Franco Platino, Kevin Gallagher, and Den Min Yeh. Byers lives in rural northern California with his wife and two sons.

First year of production: 1984
Approximate annual production: 12
Percent custom instruments: 100
Types of guitars built: Nylon-strings
Primary output: Classicals
Custom options: Elevated fingerboard, scale length

Gregory Byers
15000 Hearst Rd.
Willits, CA 95490
Phone/fax: (707) 459-4068

M. CAMPELLONE GUITARS

Influenced by the Beatles and other popular music of the mid-'60s, Mark Campellone began playing guitar at age ten. He played his father's old Stella flattop for two years before getting his first good guitar: a Gibson hollow-body electric. Eventually he began playing jazz guitar and also became interested in the archtop guitars associated with the style. He attended the Berklee College of Music and subsequently worked as a professional musician. He began building electric six-string guitars and basses in the mid-'70s, as well as repairing both electric and acoustic instruments. He built his first archtop in 1988 and quickly decided to stop playing professionally so that he could concentrate on lutherie. Inspired by the great orchestra-style instruments, Campellone's archtops are among the world's finest. Their styling, playability, high-quality materials, and excellent craftsmanship have gained the attention of archtop enthusiasts across the U.S. and abroad.

First year of production: 1978
Approximate annual production: 18
Percent custom instruments: 100
Types of guitars built: Archtops
Custom options: Body size, floating pickups, cutaway, scale length, inlays
Guitar pictured: p. 76

M. Campellone Guitars
5 Mapleville Rd.
Smithfield, RI 02828
Phone: (401) 949-3716
www.mcampellone.com

CARVIN CORP.

Carvin started building Hawaiian lap steel guitars in 1946. The line expanded to electric Spanish guitars and acoustic guitars in the early '50s. Through the '60s and '70s the company focused on electric solid-bodies and archtop acoustic-electrics. Today the Carvin custom shop offers more than 1,000 choices.

First year of production: 1946
Approximate annual production: 6,000
Percent custom instruments: 90
Types of guitars built: Steel-string flat-tops, 12-strings, nylon-strings
Custom options: Woods, inlays, finishes

Carvin Corp.
12340 World Trade Dr.
San Diego, CA 92128-3742
Phone: (858) 487-1600
Fax: (858) 487-8786
www.carvin.com

CASA MONTALVO

Casa Montalvo and Superior guitars are award-winning, highly affordable instruments produced in Mexico for George Katechis Montalvo, a master craftsman with experience in all aspects of tone production. Montalvo began repairing and selling musical instruments at the age of 12. He has studied silver- and gold-smithing, Renaissance and Baroque woodwind construction, piano soundboard technology, and the properties of strings under tension. In 1990 he started the K&S guitar company, helping to design and produce the guitars. Since 1999 he has been on his own, working with many fine Mexican guitar makers on Casa Montalvo and Superior guitars. He brought higher-quality woods, glues, finishes, and American builders and restorers to share their knowledge with the staff in Mexico. All Casa Montalvo and Superior guitars are painstakingly set up and inspected by George Montalvo at his shop in Berkeley, California. They are constructed of all solid, air-dried, aged woods, and the nylon-string instruments have graphite reinforcing bars in the necks and nitrocellulose lacquer finishes. Many professionals, including John Scofield and David Lindley, are using these instruments for performing and recording.

First year of production: 1987
Approximate annual production: 60–100
Percent custom instruments: 5
Types of guitars built: Steel-string flat-tops, 12-strings, nylon-strings, Hawaiian guitars
Primary output: Classicals and flamencos
Guitar pictured: p. 70

Casa Montalvo Guitars
2923 Adeline St.
Berkeley, CA 94703-2502

Phone: (510) 548-7538
Fax: (510) 644-2273
www.berkeleymusic.com

CHRYSALIS GUITARS

Tim White has played 12-string guitar since the age of 17. He left pre-med studies at Yale University in 1974 to study lutherie as the first apprentice to Michael Millard of Froggy Bottom Guitars. After a year, he returned to school to study insect acoustics as well as guitar acoustics under the tutelage of Dr. Daniel Haines, who developed the first carbon fiber soundboard materials and was a leading researcher in the study of tonewoods used in stringed instruments. After earning his degree, White completed two more years at Froggy Bottom to fulfill his apprenticeship. After several more years studying fine woodworking and antique repair, he opened a guitar shop in Ann Arbor, Michigan, in 1980. He founded the *Journal of Guitar Acoustics*, which he published for three years. During this time, the idea for the Chrysalis inflatable guitar was born, and a first crude prototype was built. The Chrysalis inflatable guitar is now in limited production.

First year of production: 1998
Approximate annual production: 10–20
Percent custom instruments: 80
Types of guitars built: Specialty guitars

Chrysalis Guitars
146 Lull Rd.
New Boston, NH 03070
Phone: (603) 487-2312
Fax: (603) 487-2699
www.chrysalisguitars.com

HARVEY CITRON ENTERPRISES

A guitarist, singer, bandleader, and graduate architect, Harvey Citron has been building guitars and basses since the early 1970s. He cofounded Veillette-Citron in 1975 and during that partnership's eight years built some of the finest handcrafted electric guitars, basses, and baritone guitars. As an independent luthier, Citron designed the Guild/Citron X/92 Breakaway guitar. His *Basic Guitar Setup and Repair* instructional video is available from Homespun Tapes. Today Citron builds guitars and basses in his shop in Woodstock, New York.

First year of production: 1995
Approximate annual production: 25
Percent custom instruments: 60
Types of guitars built: Steel-string flat-tops, specialty guitars
Primary output: Steel-string flattops
Custom options: Scale length, electronics, neck dimensions, string spacing

Harvey Citron Enterprises
282 Chestnut Hill Rd.
Woodstock, NY 12498

Phone: (914) 679-7138
Fax: (914) 679-3221
www.citron-guitars.com

ED CLAXTON GUITARS

While taking a music course at the University of Texas at Austin, Ed Claxton built an oud for his term project and became fascinated with the design and construction of stringed instruments. He went on to build a variety of instruments, such as the lyre, harp, hurdy-gurdy, hammer dulcimer, and bouzouki. His main interest, however, was the guitar, and in 1972 Claxton opened his first shop where he built and repaired guitars and developed the models for the instruments that he makes today. After a number of years, Claxton left Austin and pursued other areas of woodworking, such as wooden boats and custom furniture, but he always maintained an interest in the guitar. In 1994 he moved to Santa Cruz, California, and once again turned to designing and building steel-string guitars full-time.

First year of production: 1972
Approximate annual production: 16–18
Percent custom instruments: 100
Types of guitars built: Steel-string flat-tops, 12-strings, specialty guitars
Primary output: Steel-string flattops
Custom options: Woods, neck widths and shapes, bindings, purflings, rosettes
Guitar pictured: p. 20

Ed Claxton Guitars
2527-C Mission St.
Santa Cruz, CA 95060
Phone: (831) 469-5463
Fax: (831) 426-9875

COLLINGS GUITARS

A lifelong interest in guitars, tools, and machinery challenged Bill Collings to attempt some stringed-instrument building and repair in the early '70s. After almost 15 years of working on his own, he rented a 1,000-square-foot space and hired two helpers. An order for 24 custom "Gruhn" guitars (Collings had met guitar dealer George Gruhn at trade shows) helped establish him in the national market. In late 1991, a 3,200-square-foot shop was purchased. Since then the space has tripled. Collings now employs 25 full-time workers and builds more than 1,000 guitars per year. As the shop has grown and been refined, there is one thing that hasn't changed: Collings' commitment to building the finest acoustic steel-string guitars possible.

First year of production: 1975
Approximate annual production: 900
Percent custom instruments: 50
Types of guitars built: Steel-string flat-tops, archtops
Primary output: Steel-string flattops

Custom options: Woods, inlays, shaded tops
Guitar pictured: p. 43

Collings Guitars
11025 Signal Hill Dr.
Austin, TX 78737
Phone: (512) 288-7776
Fax: (512) 288-6045
www.collingsguitars.com

COMINS GUITARS

Bill Comins' journey into lutherie began in the mid-'80s while he was studying jazz guitar at Temple University in Philadelphia. As his reputation for repair and setup work grew, he found himself with a part-time business. He eventually took a job in a violin shop, where he worked for four years. During this time he met Bob Benedetto and began to tool up, with Bob's guidance and encouragement, to manufacture and refine his own line of archtop guitars. In 1996 Comins was asked to build a guitar for Scott Chinery's blue collection.

First year of production: 1994
Approximate annual production: 15–20
Percent custom instruments: 100
Types of guitars built: Archtops
Custom options: Body size, binding, alternative soundholes
Guitar pictured: p. 81

Comins Guitars
PO Box 611
Willow Grove, PA 19090-0611
Phone/fax: (215) 784-0314
www.cominsguitars.com

STEPHAN CONNOR

Stephan Connor started playing guitar and studying music when he was a teenager and went on to study classical guitar technique in Paris with Tania Chagnot. When he acquired an instrument built by Manuel Velazquez, he was astounded by its beauty and decided that he wanted to build classical guitars. After graduating from college, he attended Timeless Instruments luthiery school, where he designed and built his first classical guitar, which was strongly influenced by the Velazquez guitar. Since then he's developed his own style, tonally and aesthetically, and he now builds custom guitars featuring elaborate mosaic work.

First year of production: 1995
Approximate annual production: 12
Percent custom instruments: 100
Types of guitars built: Nylon-strings
Custom options: Body size, scale length, string spacing, woods
Guitar pictured: p. 54

Stephan Connor
681 Main St.
Waltham, MA 02452
Phone: (781) 647-9920

PAOLO CORIANI

Paolo Coriani became interested in building classical guitars in 1975. His methods combine traditional and innovative construction techniques. He pays particular attention to choosing and matching the tonewoods used in each guitar—such as red spruce, Canadian cedar, Brazilian rosewood, jacaranda, Indian rosewood, and Central American mahogany and ebony—and to careful workmanship and tone production. His instruments are inspired by the great Spanish masters of the first half of the 20th century, and he attended a course on the construction of the Spanish classical guitar given by J.L. Romanillos in 1993. In 1986 Coriani won first prize in the classical guitar category of the National Violin-Making Exhibition of Bagnacavallo, and in 1993 he won first prize at the first International Guitar Contest in Baveno.

First year of production: 1984
Approximate annual production: 12
Percent custom instruments: 25
Types of guitars built: Nylon-strings
Primary output: Classicals
Guitar pictured: p. 62

Paolo Coriani
Via Barchetta 98
41100 Modena, Italy
Phone: (39) 59-827565
Fax: (39) 522-628786
www.digicolor.net/ali/coriani

P.W. CRUMP CO.

Upon completing a biology degree at Humboldt State University in 1971, Phil Crump took the next logical step and decided to become a guitar maker. After training with Mark Platin at the Wildwood Banjo Co., the P.W. Crump Co. was established in 1975 as a repair and custom-guitar shop serving area music stores and musicians. Acoustic and electric guitars have been produced on a custom basis since the shop opened and enjoy a reputation for first-rate craftsmanship, tone, and playability. A multi-instrumentalist for over 35 years, Crump's interest in Celtic music resulted in the production of his first octave mandolin in 1987. This instrument was a synthesis of techniques and concepts from various sources: the X-brace from C.F. Martin and Co., plate-tuning ideas from the work of Carleen Hutchins and others, laminated neck construction from the great banjo makers past and present, and the pioneering work of Stefan Sobell and Rich Westerman. Crump's line of Celtic instruments also incorporates the latest innovations in truss rods, pickups, and finish technology.

First year of production: 1975
Approximate annual production: 24–36
Types of guitars built: Steel-string flattops, specialty guitars
Primary output: Steel-string flattops

P.W. Crump Co.
187 Fickle Hill Rd.

Arcata, CA 95521
Phone: (707) 826-1164
Fax: (707) 826-9530
www.pwcrumpco.com

WILLIAM CUMPIANO

William R. Cumpiano was born in Puerto Rico in 1950 and has been making guitars in the American, European, and Latin American traditions since the late '60s. He builds his guitars by hand, one and two at a time, in his Northampton, Massachusetts, studio. He also teaches his craft and writes about his field in books, magazines, and on the Web at www.cumpiano.com. He is coauthor of the premier textbook in the field, *Guitarmaking: Tradition and Technology*, and is working on a new textbook about the stringed-instrument traditions of the U.S., Caribbean, and Central and South America.

First year of production: 1974
Approximate annual production: 12–18
Percent custom instruments: 100
Types of guitars built: Steel-string flattops, 12-strings, nylon-strings, specialty guitars
Primary output: Classics and steel-string flattops
Custom options: Ergonomic designs
Guitar pictured: p. 69

William Cumpiano
8 East Hampton Rd.
Northampton, MA 01060
Phone: (413) 586-3730
Fax: (413) 584-4596
www.cumpiano.com

DAILY GUITARS

David S. Daily has been a luthier since 1976 and has built more than 300 classical guitars. His work is deeply rooted in the Spanish tradition because of his association with Antonio Marin Montero of Granada, Spain, but Daily's many years of intense experimentation and his unwillingness to accept the shortcomings of the instrument have pushed him to stretch the boundaries of the classical guitar. His guitars have been played in the most important venues and guitar competitions around the world by such notable players as Andrew York, Ernesto Tamayo, and Aliexsey Vianna. York says of Daily's guitars, "They have superior sustain, clarity, brilliance, and volume—a combination that is difficult to find in one instrument."

First year of production: 1976
Approximate annual production: 20
Types of guitars built: Steel-string flattops, nylon-strings
Primary output: Classicals
Guitar pictured: p. 57

Daily Guitars
1425 Greenbrae Dr.
Sparks, NV 89431
Phone: (775) 359-6370
Fax: (775) 359-2047
www.dailyguitars.com

J. THOMAS DAVIS

J. Thomas Davis began building guitars in a basement workshop while working on his music degree in the mid-'70s. His objective was to build a classical guitar for himself, but one of his students wanted one, and then another. Upon graduating in 1977, he moved his shop to a storefront location. By this time, he was building steel-string flattops in addition to classicals, and he began making some carved-top instruments in the early '80s. Davis' shop employs three people in the repair and service end of the business, but Davis himself performs all the work on his instruments with his own hands. Each instrument is individually made and tailored to the customer's specific desires, with an emphasis placed on the sound the customer wants.

First year of production: 1975
Approximate annual production: 8–10
Percent custom instruments: 100
Types of guitars built: Steel-string flattops, 12-strings, nylon-strings
Guitars pictured: pp. 37, 82

J. Thomas Davis
3135 N. High St.
Columbus, OH 43202
Phone: (614) 263-0264
Fax: (614) 447-0174
www.jthomasdavis.com

DEARSTONE MANDOLIN WORKS

Ray Dearstone has been making acoustic instruments, mostly mandolins, since 1980. In 1993 he founded Dearstone Mandolin Works with his brother Terry. The company specializes in custom mandolins and guitars, including acoustic-electrics, flattops, archtops, and resophonics.

First year of production: 1993
Approximate annual production: 6
Percent custom instruments: 100
Types of guitars built: Steel-string flattops, archtops, resonator guitars
Primary output: Steel-string flattops

Dearstone Mandolin Works
105 24th St.
Bristol, TN 37620
Phone/fax: (423) 968-9599
www.dearstone.com

SERGEI DE JONGE

Sergei de Jonge began his career in 1970 as an apprentice to Jean Larrivée, when Larrivée was exclusively building classical guitars. In 1971 de Jonge went to study with Patt Lister for eight months in order to get a different perspective on classical guitars. Lister was an innovative luthier with unorthodox ideas such as using lattice bracing. Although de Jonge learned much about tone from Lister, he ultimately built guitars in the German tradition he learned from Larrivée. In 1972 de Jonge started his own work

shop, where he built mostly classical guitars for the next 14 years. In 1986 he lost his shop and didn't get back into full-time guitar building until 1992, when his children got into the act. Joshia, Sagen, Rubin, and Alan de Jonge are all building guitars with their father these days, and Joshia and Sagen have established reputations in their own right. Patrick Hodgins is also working full-time in the de Jonge workshop, where about 60 guitars are completed each year.

First year of production: 1972
Approximate annual production: 60
Percent custom instruments: 50
Types of guitars built: Steel-string flattops, 12-strings, nylon-strings, specialty guitars
Primary output: Classicals
Guitars pictured: pp. 40, 61

Sergei de Jonge
883 Robson St.
Oshawa, ON L1H 4C6
Canada
Phone: (905) 576-2255
Fax: (905) 576-8399
www.myna.com/~sdejonge

DELL'ARTE INSTRUMENTS

John S. Kinnard, half owner and master luthier at Dell'Arte Instruments, grew up in San Diego, California, during the '60s. In the '70s he and Peter Webster owned Heritage Guitar Works, where Kinnard learned how to restore vintage stringed instruments. He took a sabbatical from guitars in the late 1980s to become involved in the jewelry business and believes that his time spent fabricating jewelry and cutting precious stones helped further hone his guitar-making skills. In the early '90s, Kinnard worked for Taylor Guitars and then opened a small shop under the name Finegold Guitars and Mandolins in 1996. He met longtime jazz guitarist Alain Cola in 1998. Cola was dealing in tonewoods and musical instrument parts and overseeing production of Selmer/Maccaferri-style guitars in Mexico. He was looking to improve the workmanship of his guitars when he met Kinnard, and the two joined forces in November 1998. Today Dell'Arte Instruments offers a full array of finely handcrafted stringed musical instruments.

First year of production: 1997
Approximate annual production: 200
Percent custom instruments: 10
Types of guitars built: Steel-string flattops, specialty guitars
Primary output: Maccaferri-style
Custom options: Dimensions, woods, appointments
Guitar pictured: p. 107

Dell'Arte Instruments
10020 Prospect Ave., Unit A25
Santee, CA 92071
Phone: (619) 596-7739
Fax: (619) 698-2237
www.dellarteinstruments.com

DE PAULE STRINGED INSTRUMENTS

C. Andrew De Paule was born in England and raised in South Africa. His family moved to southern California in 1957 when he was ten years old. After three and a half years in the army and two in Vietnam, De Paule moved to San Francisco in 1968, where he built his first electric guitar and started repairing guitars. In 1970 he moved to Willits, California, where he started building acoustic guitars and dulcimers and opened his first shop. For the most part he is self-taught as a luthier, although in the beginning he got his questions answered by San Francisco luthier George Peacock. De Paule started building archtop guitars in 1978, took 12 years away from the business starting in 1980, and then returned to lutherie working for Zeta Music in Oakland, California, where he helped build Strado electric violins. He left the San Francisco Bay Area in 1993 to move to Eugene, Oregon, where he continued to build instruments and taught a guitar-building class at Lane College. He now lives in Eugene, Oregon.

First year of production: 1969
Approximate annual production: 10–12
Percent custom instruments: 100
Types of guitars built: Steel-string flat-tops, nylon-strings, archtops, resonator guitars, Hawaiian guitars, specialty guitars
Primary output: Steel-string flattops and archtops
Custom options: Left-handed, cutaways, inlays, woods
Guitar pictured: p. 85

De Paule Stringed Instruments
1173 Berntzen Rd.
Eugene, OR 97402

DEVOE GUITARS

In the early 1970s, Lester DeVoe studied classical guitar in the San Francisco Bay Area. He built his first guitar for himself after studying books and the musical instrument collection of late luthier Gabriel Sousa of San Jose, California. DeVoe was primarily interested in Sousa's classical and flamenco guitar collection, which included generations of Spanish guitars dating back before Antonio de Torres' time. In 1981 legendary flamenco guitarist Sabicas discovered a DeVoe guitar in a New York City music store, and he continued to use DeVoes in concerts and recording sessions for the rest of his life. DeVoe moved to Maine in 1992 and began building instruments for Paco de Lucía. He makes regular trips to Europe in search of tonewoods and has had the pleasure of meeting some of today's greatest flamenco artists. Some of the players using his instruments are Brian Amador, Ken Andrade, Govi, Stevan Pasero, and Thomas Rhode.

First year of production: 1975
Approximate annual production: 16–20
Percent custom instruments: 75
Types of guitars built: Nylon-strings
Primary output: Flamencos, classicals
Custom options: Fingerboard width, neck shape, scale length
Guitar pictured: p. 67

DeVoe Guitars
680 Camino Roble
Nipomo, CA 93444
Phone: (805) 931-0313
www.maui.net/~rtadaki/devoe.html

DILLON GUITARS

John Dillon began building guitars in New Mexico in 1975. His mentor was master luthier Max Krimmel of Boulder, Colorado, and their informal relationship, unlike a traditional apprenticeship, allowed Dillon to make mistakes, figure things out, and develop a style of his own. Dillon now lives in rural Pennsylvania, where he operates a one-man shop specializing in custom acoustic steel-string guitars. He has built instruments for Steve Earle, Tish Hinojosa, Michael Martin Murphey, the Mavericks, Ray Kennedy, Hank Williams, Jr., and Trisha Yearwood. Dillon enjoys the whole process of working with players to design and build their ideal guitars, from selecting woods and decorative inlays, to hand-carving necks, to determining the player's ideal string spacing. Because he is not limited by mass-production constraints, he can do just about anything a client wants.

First year of production: 1975
Approximate annual production: 6–10
Percent custom instruments: 100
Types of guitars built: Steel-string flat-tops, 12-strings
Primary output: Steel-string flattops
Guitar pictured: p. 49

Dillon Guitars
17 Stewart Ln.
Bloomsburg, PA 17815
Phone: (570) 784-7552
Fax: (570) 784-8328
www.picasso.net/dillon

D'LECO GUITARS

James W. Dale began building guitars in 1953 in his high school woodworking class. He grew up in a musical family and was exposed to many fine musicians and instruments as a child. His father was a cabinetmaker, so building guitars came naturally to Dale. After his father died in 1991, Dale fulfilled their shared dream of building instruments for a living, and he considers his work a memorial to his father's memory.

First year of production: 1991
Approximate annual production: 12–16
Percent custom instruments: 75
Types of guitars built: Archtops, specialty guitars
Primary output: Archtops
Custom options: Neck profile, f-hole options, size, scale length, inlays, etc.
Guitar pictured: p. 74

D'Leco Guitars
2000 N.W. 15th St.
Oklahoma City, OK 73106
Phone/fax: (405) 524-0448
www.charliechristian.com

DOOLIN GUITARS

Mike Doolin has been a professional guitarist since 1974 and a luthier since 1985. His background in music performance, software engineering, and graphic arts contribute to the design of instruments that are both highly functional and strikingly beautiful. His instruments all feature his double-cutaway design, which provides clear access to all frets. Doolin's models include a 22-fret steel-string and a 19-fret nylon-string. "An added benefit of the double cutaway," he says, "is the consistency of tone it produces in all registers. Because all the frets are on the neck (rather than over the body), the high register has a ringing, harp-like sustain that blends perfectly with the lower register." Doolin works alone, handcrafting each instrument individually.

First year of production: 1996
Approximate annual production: 20
Percent custom instruments: 40
Types of guitars built: Steel-string flat-tops, nylon-strings
Primary output: Double cutaways
Custom options: Woods, scale length, neck profile, number of strings, pickups, ergonomic body profiles
Guitar pictured: p. 50

Doolin Guitars
3775 S.E. Stephens St.
Portland, OR 97214
Phone: (503) 236-2424
Fax: (503) 236-1976
www.doolinguitars.com

DRAGGE GUITARS

Peter Dragge studied guitar building with Ervin Somogyi in 1981 and 1982. He has built guitars for Rickie Lee Jones, Steve Lukather, Darcy Johnstone, Dean Parks, and Mark Casstevens. He is known for the Dragge Duo-Sphere, an instrument that incorporates both top and back plates as sections of perfect spheres. The design improves volume, projection, balance, and dynamics.

First year of production: 1982
Approximate annual production: 6
Percent custom instruments: 100
Types of guitars built: Steel-string flat-tops, nylon-strings
Custom options: Rare woods, Dragge Duo Sphere plate design, inlays
Guitar pictured: p. 39

Dragge Guitars
816 Foothill Ln.
Ojai, CA 93023
Phone: (805) 646-9986

MICHAEL DUNN

In 1966 Michael Dunn began a three-year apprenticeship in guitar making under maestros Jose Orti and Jose Ferrer at George Bowden's workshop in Mallorca, Spain. A solid grounding in the Spanish tradition of construction and aesthetics has allowed him the freedom to experiment with artistic expression and sound projection while respecting the craft's tried-and-true tenets of proportion, balance, and function. Early on in his career, he became fascinated with the music of Django Reinhardt and the guitars he played. Dunn has been playing Hot Club–style music and constructing guitars based on the Maccaferri and Selmer designs since the late '60s. These instruments constitute 90 percent of his output. He has worked within this tradition but has chosen not to make carbon copies of the originals, constructing contemporary renditions of these guitars and always bearing in mind the need to reproduce that certain sound and timbre reminiscent of the 1930s. His approach to the instrument is as much from a player's viewpoint as a luthier's.

First year of production: 1968
Approximate annual production: 25
Percent custom instruments: 20
Types of guitars built: Nylon-strings, archtops, Hawaiian guitars, specialty guitars
Primary output: Maccaferri-style
Custom options: Woods, neck width
Guitar pictured: p. 106

Michael Dunn
708 Third Ave.
New Westminster, BC V3M 1N7
Canada
Phone: (604) 524-1943
www.michaeldunnguitars.com

DUNWELL GUITARS

Alan Dunwell has been building guitars on a part-time basis for many years and has been building professionally since 1995. Dunwell runs his one-man shop out of his home in the Rocky Mountains near Nederland, Colorado, and builds his guitars one at a time. He is a member of the Guild of American Luthiers and the Association of Stringed Instrument Artisans. His emphasis is on acoustic flattop guitars for fingerpicking and flatpicking, and alternative woods are his specialty. He offers 000, OM, deep-body OM, and dreadnought models. All his instruments are plate-tuned and constructed in such a way as to get the most from the individual woods. Dunwell is also working on two F-style mandolin models, the

Redbone and the Bluetick, and is experimenting with indigenous woods for a Colorado guitar.

First year of production: 1996
Approximate annual production: 3–6
Percent custom instruments: 100
Types of guitars built: Steel-string flat-tops, 12-strings
Primary output: Steel-string flattops
Custom options: Woods, binding, purfling, inlays
Guitar pictured: p. 13

Dunwell Guitars
1891 CR 68-J MSR
Nederland, CO 80466
Phone: (303) 939-8870
www.peaknet.org/webpages/dunwell

WILLIAM EATON

Musician and composer William Eaton designs and builds the unique instruments he performs with, such as the 31-string O'ele'n and the 16-string lyre. He has written music for film, video, chamber orchestras, dance ensembles, and musicals and has released numerous CDs, including *Tracks We Leave* (solo) and *Carry the Gift* (with Native American flutist R. Carlos Nakai). In 1971 Eaton apprenticed with the late John Roberts, and he has been an administrator and teacher at the Roberto-Venn School of Luthiery in Phoenix, Arizona, since 1974. His newest instrument, the lyraharp guitar, was designed to incorporate Eaton's accumulated knowledge of building guitars, harp guitars, and lyres with the sophistication of Roland's synthesizer technology, permitting voicings for nearly every existing musical instrument. The lyraharp has had a profound and expansive influence on Eaton's musical directions.

First year of production: 1976
Approximate annual production: 1
Percent custom instruments: 100
Types of guitars built: Specialty guitars
Primary output: Harp guitars and other multi-stringed instruments
Guitar pictured: p. 102

William Eaton
Roberto-Venn School of Luthiery
4011 S. 16th St.
Phoenix, AZ 85040
Phone: (602) 243-1179
Fax: (602) 304-1175
www.roberto-venn.com

GILA EBAN GUITARS

Gila Eban has been building and repairing guitars for professional and amateur musicians since the late '70s. She pursues innovation and musical acoustics research, is a strong adherent of traditional lutherie practices, and studies the interrelation of tradition and innovation. Her work and study with late archtop builder James D'Aquisto has greatly informed her building and led her to more refined approaches to classical guitar setup

and playability, an issue about which she is somewhat of an activist.

First year of production: 1979
Approximate annual production: 6
Percent custom instruments: 100
Types of guitars built: Nylon-strings
Primary output: Classicals
Custom options: Scale length, soundboard designs, rosette, woods, tuning machines
Guitar pictured: p. 67

Gila Eban Guitars
PO Box 95
Riverside, CT 06878
Phone: (203) 625-8307

EICHELBAUM CUSTOM GUITARS

David Eichelbaum has been repairing guitars in his California workshop since 1991 and building his own line of steel-string flattops since 1995. Essentially self-taught as a luthier, he nonetheless considers the continual advice and direction from good friends Kevin Ryan and Jim Olson integral to his design and building processes. He offers three styles of guitars: the Grand Concert model, which is especially suited for fingerstyle playing; the Sierra Orchestra model, which is a terrific all-around guitar; and a deeper-bodied version of the Sierra designed for maximum volume. He's working on a new Jumbo model designed to suit the needs of those looking for something closer to a dreadnought. All Eichelbaum guitars are constructed with the finest woods and finished in high-gloss nitrocellulose lacquer. Only wood binding and purflings are used. Modern neck-joining techniques and production methods are combined with traditional lutherie techniques to create a musically pleasing instrument that will last for generations to come. Many custom woods are available, as are inlay designs by Larry Robinson.

First year of production: 1994
Approximate annual production: 10–12
Percent custom instruments: 100
Types of guitars built: Steel-string flat-tops, 12-strings
Primary output: Steel-string flattops
Custom options: Inlays, trim, neck shape

Eichelbaum Custom Guitars
1735 Mountain Ave.
Santa Barbara, CA 93101
Phone: (805) 563-6028
www.escribes.com/eichelbaum

JEFFREY R. ELLIOTT

In 1964 a chance visit to Richard Schneider's workshop in Detroit, Michigan, opened the door to the world of lutherie for Jeffrey R. Elliott. Two years later he began a six-year apprenticeship with Schneider. In 1973 he moved to Portland, Oregon, where he shares life and lutherie with

his partner Cynthia H. Burton. In 1975 he wrote and coproduced the color slide presentation *The Handcrafted Classic Guitar,* which accompanied one of his guitars in the Smithsonian Institution's 1978–79 Renwick Gallery exhibit The Harmonious Craft, in Washington, D.C. Elliott has been an active member of the Guild of American Luthiers since 1975 and has also taught guitar making privately since 1972. Elliott guitars are constructed in the Torres/Hauser design tradition and are tailored to the individual. Elliott considers the match between the player and the instrument crucial and works with each customer to create an instrument that is well-suited musically, physically, and aesthetically. He makes a limited number of guitars each year and his clients include Julian Bream, Burl Ives, Earl Klugh, Leo Kottke, and Ralph Towner.

First year of production: 1966
Approximate annual production: 6–8
Percent custom instruments: 100
Types of guitars built: Steel-string flat-tops, 12-strings, nylon-strings, specialty guitars
Primary output: Classicals
Custom options: Woods, cutaways, additional strings, French polish
Guitar pictured: p. 58

Jeffrey R. Elliott
2812 S.E. 37th Ave.
Portland, OR 97202
Phone: (503) 233-0836
www.maui.net/~rtadaki/elliott.html

EVERETT GUITARS

Kent Everett began building guitars in 1977 and has had a guitar in the works ever since. Primarily a self-taught luthier, Everett worked for and later owned Atlanta, Georgia's premier repair shop, the Atlanta Guitar Works, in the 1980s. Despite the fact that he spent 50 hours per week repairing and restoring guitars, he still found evening and weekend time to follow his passion for building and produced approximately ten instruments per year. He built a variety of archtop guitars, semi-hollow and solid-body electric guitars, acoustics, Dobros, and mandolins, and he received a patent for his electric guitar design in 1988. In 1990 he closed the Atlanta Guitar Works and opened Everett Guitars, a one-man shop dedicated to building high-end acoustic guitars. By the mid-1990s he was building 54 guitars per year for dealers across the United States, Germany, and Japan.

First year of production: 1977
Approximate annual production: 50
Percent custom instruments: 50
Types of guitars built: Steel-string flat-tops, nylon-strings
Primary output: Steel-string flattops
Guitar pictured: p. 17

Everett Guitars
2338 Johnson Ferry Rd.
Atlanta, GA 30341
Phone: (770) 451-2485
www.everettguitars.com

EVERGREEN MOUNTAIN

In 1971 Jerry Nolte built his first stringed instrument, hand-split from an old-growth cedar log. He has been building and repairing instruments for a living ever since. Although his instruments have changed greatly in quality as his craftsmanship has developed, he still primarily uses hand tools to bring each individual instrument to its full potential. He builds five sizes of acoustic guitars: a small New Yorker size, a fuller-bodied studio size, a mid-sized concert model, a large-bodied auditorium, and a super-jumbo bass. He also builds A-style archtop mandolins. The majority of the woods he uses are sawed or split directly from selected trees and air-dried for three to six years before they're used. Nolte is partial to using cedar soundboards and American black walnut backs and sides. Some of his instruments' unique features include wood pickguards, highly arched backs, wood binding, three-piece neck construction, pierced and carved designs around the soundhole, and master-grade violin varnishes.

First year of production: 1979
Approximate annual production: 10
Percent custom instruments: 100
Types of guitars built: Steel-string flattops, 12-strings, nylon-strings, specialty guitars
Primary output: Steel-string flattops
Guitar pictured: p. 21

Evergreen Mountain
1608 Jasper
Cove, OR 97824
Phone: (541) 568-4687
www.eoni.com/~emi

EVERLY GUITARS

Robert Steinegger first became involved with stringed instruments in the early 1960s while he was in high school in Paradise, California. He met guitar builder and designer Arthur Overholtzer in 1969 and began building classical and then steel-string guitars. He worked at Intermountain Guitar and Banjo, where he met and did some repair work for Phil Everly. Steinegger relocated to Portland, Oregon, in 1976 and became affiliated with the Twelfth Fret Guitar Shop. In 1981 Everly commissioned him to build an updated, improved version of the highly collectible Everly Brothers guitar, which Everly and his brother used during the 1960s. The brothers have used the resulting Ike Everly Model exclusively ever since. Steinegger also builds Martin-style guitars, including a Brazilian rosewood D-45, a custom Delta X (based on the 00-42), and the Everly Tropicbird guitar, which looks like a Martin style 28 but with the Everly shape. Steinegger has built instruments for George Harrison, Pat Alger, Craig Carothers, David Grisman, and Paul McCartney. Perhaps his most spectacular creation was the Everly D-50, which was built at the request of Phil Everly as a gift for his brother Don's 50th birthday. The D-50 has ebony back and sides and is bound and inlaid with nearly a pound of solid, 14-karat gold.

First year of production: 1983
Approximate annual production: 6–8
Percent custom instruments: 60
Types of guitars built: Steel-string flattops, 12-strings
Primary output: Steel-string flattops
Custom options: Cutaways, woods

Everly Guitars
PO Box 25304
Portland, OR 97298
Phone: (503) 292-8736
www.everlyguitars.com

FINE RESOPHONIC

Fine Resophonic Guitars started in 1990 when Mike Lewis and Pierre Avocat teamed up to hand-build replicas of prewar National guitars: triplate and single-cone resonator guitars, ukuleles, and mandolins. Each instrument uses the specifications of the original prewar design. Fine Resophonic also designs and builds a variety of wood-body guitars and resonator instruments using such materials as koa and flamed maple. The instruments are finished with high-gloss nitrocellulose lacquer, and the resonator cones are hand-spun using the same alloys used by the original companies. Noted performers who play Fine Resophonic guitars include Eric Clapton, Louisiana Red, and Michael Messer.

First year of production: 1988
Approximate annual production: 15–20
Percent custom instruments: 50
Types of guitars built: Resonator guitars
Primary output: Resonator guitars, baritones
Custom options: Neck shapes, woods, slotted headstocks, engraving
Guitar pictured: p. 91

Fine Resophonic
3 Voie Coypel
94400 Vitry Sur Seine
France
Phone/fax: (33) 146778617
www.fineresophonic.fr.st

FLEISHMAN INSTRUMENTS

Harry Fleishman has been building custom guitars since the early 1970s. He also teaches guitar design and building in small-class settings at his school, the Luthiers School of the Rockies, and is former director of the American School of Lutherie. In addition to designing guitars for other companies, Fleishman designs tools and fixtures for the lutherie community. As an active member of the Guild of American Luthiers, he has lectured on acoustic guitar amplification and chaired a panel on unconventional acoustic guitar design. He continues his research and experiments in asymmetric design, multi-soundport, and multi-tonewood instruments.

First year of production: 1974
Approximate annual production: 10
Percent custom instruments: 100
Types of guitars built: Steel-string flattops, 12-strings, nylon-strings, specialty guitars
Primary output: Steel-string flattops
Custom options: Asymmetric, multi-soundhole, multi-tonewood, MIDI, inlays
Guitar pictured: p. 19

Fleishman Instruments
4500 Whitney Pl.
Boulder, CO 80303
Phone: (303) 499-1614
www.fleishmaninstruments.com

FONTANILLA GUITARS

A San Francisco, California, native, Allan Fontanilla is a self-taught luthier who builds between eight and ten classical guitars per year. He built his first instrument in his spare time in 1987 while earning his B.A. in music at the San Francisco Conservatory of Music. He now devotes most of his time to building and repairing guitars, and his custom-built instruments range in style from conservative to nontraditional. Fontanilla has exhibited his guitars at the 1997 Healdsburg Guitar Festival and the 1997, 1998, and 1999 meetings of the Guitar Foundation of America (GFA). His instruments have been featured in *Acoustic Guitar* and *Fingerstyle Guitar* magazines.

First year of production: 1987
Approximate annual production: 8–10
Percent custom instruments: 40
Types of guitars built: Nylon-strings
Primary output: Classicals

Fontanilla Guitars
PO Box 31423
San Francisco, CA 94131
Phone: (415) 642-9375
www.fontanilla.com

FOUILLEUL

Self-taught guitar maker Jean-Marie Fouilleul began building instruments in 1978. He met a Spanish guitar maker who gave him a few plans and in 1983 he settled in Rennes (Brittany) and began building guitars for Europe's finest players (in Belgium, Germany, Switzerland, etc.). He has also sold instruments in Japan and Singapore. In 1998 Fouilleul moved to the country, settling near Mont St. Michel.

First year of production: 1979
Approximate annual production: 18
Percent custom instruments: 90
Types of guitars built: Steel-string flattops, nylon-strings
Primary output: Classicals
Guitar pictured: p. 63

Fouilleul
La Villate
35270 Cuguen
France
Phone: (33) 2-99-733983
Fax: (33) 2-99-733984

CFOX GUITARS

Charles Fox enjoys an international reputation as a luthier, educator, and consultant in the field of guitar building. His original design concepts and construction techniques are widely used by leading guitar makers and factories around the world. Fox began building guitars in 1968 and since then has built every type, working both as an independent luthier and as head of his own guitar production shop. In 1973 Fox founded the first school of guitar builders in North America, the Guitar Research and Design Center, where many of today's established luthiers were introduced to their craft. In subsequent years he founded and directed the American School of Lutherie in Healdsburg, California. CFox Guitars is the product of Fox's decades of experience as an artist, craftsman, and teacher.

First year of production: 1997
Approximate annual production: 350
Percent custom instruments: 75
Types of guitars built: Steel-string flattops, 12-strings, nylon-strings
Primary output: Steel-strings
Guitar pictured: p. 42

CFox Guitars
449 Allan Ct.
Healdsburg, CA 95448
Phone: (707) 433-8228
Fax: (707) 433-8180
www.cfoxguitars.com

FRAME WORKS GUITARS

Frame Works Guitars' Frank Krocker first aspired to be a professional jazz guitarist, but his interest soon moved to building fine guitars. After minimal training in the craft, he set up his own workshop in Burghausen, Germany, in 1986. At first he built electric guitars, steel-string acoustics, archtops, and classicals, but his focus shifted to classical guitars. He begins all of his instruments with a very clear vision of the desired tonal qualities. In the past he experimented with body shapes and sizes, scale lengths, and bracing systems, but his work since 1992 has been traditional, using a slightly modified Torres/Hauser design. A typical Frame Works guitar is built of Indian rosewood back and sides, a spruce top, a Honduras cedar (or cedrella) neck, an ebony fingerboard, and flamed maple binding and is finished with 15 coats of hand-rubbed oil. All of Krocker's guitars feature slightly domed tops, which allows him to make the bracing thinner so the instruments can be more sensitive to string vibration. The Frame guitar is an acoustic-electric Krocker recently designed for travel. Many professional players use the Frame guitar, including Pat Metheny, Andrew York, Gilberto Gil, and Ralph Towner.

First year of production: 1986
Approximate annual production: 150–200
Percent custom instruments: 25
Types of guitars built: Nylon-strings, specialty guitars
Primary output: Nylon-strings

Frame Works Guitars
Spitalgasse 202
84489 Burghausen
Germany
Phone: (49) 8677-912870
Fax: (49) 8677-912872
www.frameworks-guitars.com

FROGGY BOTTOM GUITARS

Michael Millard learned woodworking as a boat builder in New England. He began playing guitar at age 13 and was a student of Reverend Gary Davis. His first experience as a luthier was in the New York shop of Michael Gurian, where he began as a builder and then became shop foreman. He left Gurian and started Froggy Bottom Guitars in 1994, taking on Andrew Mueller as a full-time partner. They build about 100 guitars per year and sell them both directly to players and through a worldwide dealer network. While Froggy Bottom guitars are built within a traditional framework, each instrument is unique in order to meet the needs of the player. Several of the craftspeople who have worked for Millard over the years have gone on to become well-known builders in their own right. Millard has also consulted for some of the larger manufacturers' design departments, designing, for example, the original Santa Fe guitar for Takamine.

First year of production: 1970
Approximate annual production: 125
Percent custom instruments: 30
Types of guitars built: Steel-string flattops, 12-strings, specialty guitars
Primary output: Steel-string flattops
Guitar pictured: p. 27

Froggy Bottom Guitars
198 Timson Hill Rd.
Newfane, VT 05345
Phone: (802) 348-6665
Fax: (802) 348-7445
www.froggybottomguitars.com

FUKUOKA MUSICAL INSTRUMENTS

First year of production: 1993
Approximate annual production: 20
Percent custom instruments: 100
Types of guitars built: Steel-string flat-tops, nylon-strings, archtops, Hawaiian guitars
Custom options: Neck and fingerboard shapes, inlays

Fukuoka Musical Instruments
1-23-17 Kichijojiminamicho
Tokyo 180-0003
Japan
Phone/fax: (81) 422-72-1381

FYLDE GUITARS

Roger Bucknall built his first guitar at age nine and was building acoustic guitars for such noted players as Gordon Giltrap, Martin Carthy, and Bert Jansch by the time he was in his early 20s. In 1973 he began building guitars under the name Fylde, the name given to the west coast of Lancashire in northern England, where Robin Hood is rumored to have escaped when fleeing the Sheriff of Nottingham. By the late 1970s Fylde had captured a strong worldwide market, especially in the United States, where players like Al Di Meola and Stanley Clarke were playing Fyldes. In addition to acoustic guitars, Fylde manufactures a range of Celtic instruments, including mandolins, bouzoukis, mandolas, and citterns. Custom instruments have always been a fundamental part of Bucknall's business.

First year of production: 1973
Approximate annual production: 200
Percent custom instruments: 20
Types of guitars built: Steel-string flat-tops, 12-strings
Primary output: Steel-string flattops
Custom options: Woods, inlays, bindings, cutaways, neck shapes, fingerboard width, etc.
Guitar pictured: p. 34

Fylde Guitars
Hartness Rd.
Gilwilly Industrial Estate
Penrith, Cumbria
CA11 9BN, United Kingdom
Phone: (44) 1768-891515
Fax: (44) 1768-868998
www.fyldeguitars.com

GABRIEL'S GUITAR WORKSHOP

Gabriel Ochoteco worked as a professional musician in the late '60s and early '70s and then apprenticed with classical guitar maker Michael Wichman in Hamburg, Germany, in 1975. He moved to Queensland, Australia, in 1984 and established Gabriel's Guitar Workshop in the center of Brisbane. He regularly builds experimental instruments in order to test new materials and technology

and incorporates the successful aspects into future instruments.

First year of production: 1979
Approximate annual production: 10
Percent custom instruments: 20
Types of guitars built: Steel-string flattops, 12-strings, nylon-strings, specialty guitars
Custom options: Electronics, multi-strings, neck width

Gabriel's Guitar Workshop
115 Gotha St.
Fortitude Valley
Brisbane, Queensland 4006
Australia
Phone: (617) 3257-3297

J.W. GALLAGHER AND SON

J.W. Gallagher first began woodworking as a cabinetmaker in Wartrace, Tennessee, in 1939. By 1965 he was constructing guitars exclusively. Don Gallagher, the fifth generation of Gallaghers to be born in Wartrace, was born in 1947 and grew up working in his father's shop. In the early 1960s he assisted his father in the development of the family business and assumed responsibility for operating the business in 1976. Gallagher guitars are built in very limited numbers. From 1965 to 1990, only 2,064 guitars were made, which is indicative of the time and care given to each instrument. There is no substitute for fine craftsmanship in a musical instrument. The workmanship on all Gallagher guitars is the same, regardless of the price or model. The difference in cost of the various models is governed by the cost of materials and the amount and type of trim used. The Gallaghers have continuously improved on their instruments over the years by developing better technical procedures, building a large inventory of well-seasoned woods, perfecting wood-curing processes, refining designs, and listening to what players have to say.

First year of production: 1965
Approximate annual production: 80–100
Percent custom instruments: 70
Types of guitars built: Steel-string flattops, 12-strings, nylon-strings
Primary output: Steel-string flattops
Guitar pictured: p. 51

J.W. Gallagher and Son
7 Main St.
Wartrace, TN 37183
Phone/fax: (931) 389-6455
www.gallagherguitar.com

GALLOUP GUITARS

Bryan Galloup has more than 20 years of experience restoring and repairing acoustic guitars, electric guitars, and basses, and his methods are on the cutting edge. Students from around the world have attended Galloup's Guitar Hospital to study under him, and his techniques for resetting necks,

cutting frets, and replacing bridges and bridge plates have been featured in the Guild of American Luthiers' quarterly publication *American Lutherie*. Galloup also teaches guitar building and serves as repair and modification columnist for the Association of Stringed Instrument Artisans' quarterly magazine *Guitarmaker*. Galloup currently builds two models, Northern Lights and the Big Mitten. His guitars feature high-quality tonewoods (including spectacular bearclaw Sitka spruce tops), all-wood bindings, and cutaways.

First year of production: 1994
Approximate annual production: 100
Percent custom instruments: 15
Types of guitars built: Steel-string flattops
Custom options: Woods, cutaways, 12 or 14 frets

Galloup Guitars
10495 Northland Dr.
Big Rapids, MI 49307
Phone: (231) 796-5611
Fax: (231) 796-3837
www.galloupguitars.com

GAMBLE AND O'TOOLE

Arnie Gamble and Erin O'Toole began building classical and steel-string guitars in 1974. Gamble handles the design and construction of the instruments, and O'Toole focuses on the inlays. Each of their instruments is built with a particular playing style in mind so that the needs of the player always come first. Multi-instrumentalist Gamble studied classical, finger-style, and flatpicking guitar before getting into guitar building. He also works as a repairer and restorer of instruments and is an authorized repairer for C.F. Martin and Co., Taylor, Guild, and Fender. O'Toole's artistic talents include illustration and graphic design.

First year of production: 1980
Approximate annual production: 4
Types of guitars built: Steel-string flattops, 12-strings, nylon-strings
Guitar pictured: p. 60

Gamble and O'Toole
PO Box 188255
Sacramento, CA 95818
Phone: (916) 448-8339
Fax: (916) 441-0255
www.ns.net/~eotoole

STEVE GANZ GUITARS

Steve Ganz made his first guitar in 1970 and his second in 1994. He has been building custom instruments since 1998, including left-handed guitars, eight-strings, and the occasional classical six-string. He has been influenced by the work of fellow Bellingham, Washington, luthiers John Rollins and Dake Traphagen, and Alieksey Viana plays one of his eight-strings.

First year of production: 1995
Approximate annual production: 12
Percent custom instruments: 50
Types of guitars built: Nylon-strings
Primary output: Classicals
Guitar pictured: p. 99

Steve Ganz Guitars
3629 Illinois Lane
Bellingham, WA 98226
Phone: (360) 647-0639
www.geocities.com/sganz_guitars

GIBSON ACOUSTIC GUITARS

The Gibson Acoustic custom shop is located within the Gibson Montana acoustic guitar plant in Bozeman, Montana. It is staffed with some of Gibson's finest luthiers, who work in the tradition handed down by a dynasty of Gibson builders that began with Orville Gibson in 1894. Led by master luthier Ren Ferguson, the Gibson Acoustic custom shop offers historic Gibson replicas, one-of-a-kind orders, museum and art guitars, and a wide range of highly ornate editions of Gibson's famous acoustics, such as the SJ-200, Hummingbird, and Dove. The custom shop's most ornate guitars have sold for as much as $60,000 and are considered to be some of the most cherished works of art in the world.

First year of production: 1989
Approximate annual production: 10,000
Percent custom instruments: 4
Types of guitars built: Steel-string flat-tops, 12-strings
Primary output: Steel-string flattops
Guitar pictured: p. 33

Gibson Acoustic Guitars
1894 Orville Way
Bozeman, MT 59718
Phone: (406) 587-4117
Fax: (406) 587-9109
www.gibson.com/acoustics

WILLIAM GILBERT GUITARS

William J. Gilbert was his father John Gilbert's sole apprentice after he graduated from college. He has been responsible for all production of Gilbert guitars since mid-1991. He has continued to develop the design of Gilbert instruments and recently began expanding the range of custom features offered.

First year of production: 1986
Approximate annual production: 10
Percent custom instruments: 100
Types of guitars built: Nylon-strings, specialty guitars
Primary output: Nylon-strings

William Gilbert Guitars
5760 Forked Horn Pl.
Paso Robles, CA 93446
Phone/fax: (805) 239-9080

GOLD TONE

Gold Tone banjos and Banjitars are

hand-crafted in Florida with carefully selected woods, excellent finishes, quality hardware, and tight-fitting parts. Gold Tone offers 18 different models, including bluegrass banjos, travelers, open-backs, long-necks, tenors, plectrums, Banjitars (six-string banjos for guitarists), Banjo-basses, and Mandobanjos. Banjitars are available in four models: the six-string GT-500 with maple rim, resonator, and neck and rosewood radiused fingerboard; the GT-750, which provides more acoustic volume and sustain; the Banjitar 12-string; and the lightweight Banjitar. They all feature heavy-duty stainless-steel tailpieces, bone nuts, chrome-plated hardware, two-way adjustable truss rods, and sealed-gear tuning machines.

First year of production: 1993
Approximate annual production: 400
Percent custom instruments: 25
Types of guitars built: Specialty guitars
Primary output: Banjos

Gold Tone
3554 S. Hopkins Ave.
Titusville, FL 32780-5681
Phone: (321) 264-1970
Fax: (321) 269-4910
www.nbbd.com/goldtone

JAMES GOODALL GUITARS

James Goodall's background in mechanics, woodworking, and design helps him in his endeavor to build the finest acoustic guitars. He got his start in instrument building alongside such noted southern California luthiers as Greg Deering, Geoff Stelling, and Larry and Kim Breedlove. By 1978 his solo guitar-making operation was in full swing. In 1981 he moved to Mendocino, California, where he turned out about 40 instruments per year, and in 1992 he moved to his current location in Kailua-Kona, Hawaii. He now employs five workers and ships six instruments per week. Despite the increased production, Goodall remains driven by his commitment to high quality and rich, harmonic tone. The unique shape of Goodall's instruments date back to his first guitar, a modified jumbo with a distinctly rounded shape. Goodall guitars are unique on the inside as well, with soundboards and bracing patterns that depart radically from the traditional X-bracing approach. The thickness of the tops are graduated so that the soundboards flex more near the edges and produce a deeper, more fundamental tone. This feature combined with nonscalloped braces results in brilliant harmonic overtones and a three-dimensional quality of sound.

First year of production: 1972
Approximate annual production: 340

Percent custom instruments: 100
Types of guitars built: Steel-string flat-tops, 12-strings, nylon-strings
Primary output: Steel-string flattops
Guitar pictured: p. 18

James Goodall Guitars
73-4786 Kanalani St., Bay 1
Kailua-Kona, HI 96740
Phone: (808) 329-8237
Fax: (808) 329-2708
www.goodallguitars.com

OSKAR GRAF

Since 1970 Oskar Graf has been building stringed instruments for an exclusive and appreciative group of musicians. He grew up in Berlin, Germany, apprenticed as a cabinetmaker, and studied design. He immigrated to Toronto, Canada, where he was introduced to the musicians and vibrant music scene of the '70s and became interested in building instruments. Graf began crafting dulcimers and quickly turned his attention to designing and building guitars. With his formal design background and his roots in the European crafts tradition, Graf brings a unique approach to guitar building. Flawless workmanship, understated detailing, and graceful lines reflect the tonal harmony and balance of his instruments. Working on two guitars at a time, he invests more than 100 hours into each instrument. He hand-shapes necks, carves braces, and planes and tunes each top and back to enhance resonance. During his long career, Graf has built more than 300 guitars and numerous other instruments, mostly custom orders. His classical and steel-string guitars are valued by musicians for performance and studio work. They are also featured in the collection of the Canadian Museum of Civilization and in the music faculties of several universities.

First year of production: 1973
Approximate annual production: 14–16
Percent custom instruments: 75
Types of guitars built: Steel-string flat-tops, 12-strings, nylon-strings, specialty guitars
Guitar pictured: p. 29

Oskar Graf
PO Box 2502
Clarendon, ON K0H 1J0
Canada
Phone: (613) 279-2610
web.ctsolutions.com/grafguitars

AARON GREEN

Aaron Green began building guitars in 1990 under Alan Carruth, with whom he studied for three years. He currently shares a shop in Waltham, Massachusetts, with luthier Stephan Connor. He has built guitars for Dennis Koster, Roberto Rios, and many teachers at the University of Rhode Island, the University of New

Hampshire, Dartmouth University, the Berklee College of Music, and the American Institute of Guitar in New York City. Green's commissions include a cedar guitar for Andrew Nitkin, director of the American Institute of Guitar, commemorating the school's 25th anniversary and a European maple and spruce guitar for the folks at La Bella strings.

First year of production: 1990
Approximate annual production: 12
Percent custom instruments: 100
Types of guitars built: Nylon-strings
Primary output: Classicals and flamencos
Guitar pictured: p. 71

Aaron Green
681 Main St.
Waltham, MA 02452
Phone: (781) 647-9920

GRIFFIN STRING INSTRUMENTS

Kim Griffin was introduced to the sound of beautiful instruments by classical violinist Virginia Farmer, who was a neighbor when he was growing up. He got his first guitar (a Harmony flattop) at the age of nine and then graduated to a Guild. He began repairing fiddles and guitars in 1975 and attended Charles Fox and George Morris' School of Guitar Research and Design in Vermont in 1977. Griffin builds hammer dulcimers, banjos, and mandolins as well as four different kinds of guitars in his cozy Greenwich, New York, workshop, usually completing between 12 and 16 instruments per year. He varies his bracing patterns and tonewood combinations depending on the feel of the individual top he's working with in order to identify and accentuate the unique potential of each instrument. He offers custom-built necks, a variety of tonewood combinations, and custom inlay work.

First year of production: 1976
Approximate annual production: 12
Percent custom instruments: 90
Types of guitars built: Steel-string flat-tops, 12-strings, nylon-strings, specialty guitars
Primary output: Steel-string flattops
Guitar pictured: p. 33

Griffin String Instruments
Route 113
Greenwich, NY 12834
Phone: (518) 695-5382
www.museweb.com/griffin

GRIMES GUITARS

Since the early 1970s, the focus of Steve Grimes' lutherie career has been the archtop guitar. After he moved to Hawaii in 1982, however, Grimes met Keola Beamer, a master slack-key guitarist in the old Hawaiian ki ho' alu style and collaborated with him on a

double-soundhole flattop guitar design that resulted in the Beamer and Hapa models. In 1991 Grimes teamed up with Ned Steinberger to produce a stress-free flattop guitar, in which the string tension is applied to a tailpiece rather than the soundboard, thereby increasing sustain and volume. He has designed guitars for Cort Guitars (the Larry Coryell model) and Ibanez (the George Benson model). Grimes has built over 250 archtop guitars and 135 flattops for such artists as George Benson, Larry Coryell, Leo Kottke, Keola Beamer, Walter Becker, Steve Miller, Pat Simmons, and Scott Chinery.

First year of production: 1974
Approximate annual production: 20
Percent custom instruments: 100
Types of guitars built: Steel-string flattops, 12-strings, nylon-strings
Primary output: Archtops
Custom options: Woods, inlays, bindings
Guitars pictured: pp. 49, 85

Grimes Guitars
755-G Kamehameiki Rd.
Kula, HI 96790
Phone/fax: (808) 878-2076
www.grimesguitars.com

GRUEN ACOUSTIC GUITARS

Paul Gruen has played guitar since he was a child, and woodworking in the Gruen family spans at least four generations. Gruen also has a scientific background and has studied guitar acoustics. He began building guitars with Massachusetts luthiers Alan Carruth and Thomas Knatt, with whom he also studied plate tuning and modal analysis. Although he has built conventional steel-string guitars, Gruen's passion is a new type of guitar of his own design that he believes has more presence and projection than a flattop and more versatility than an archtop or a Selmer-type guitar. Gruen's EQ guitars feature five soundholes: four ovals where f-holes traditionally appear on archtops, plus a small round center soundhole. Gruen supplies each customer with two wooden stoppers that can be used to plug any of the four oval soundholes. The result is a rainbow of different tonal balances. The EQ can be built with a variety of woods and in a range of dimensions to accommodate each customer's desires.

First year of production: 1999
Approximate annual production: 10–20
Percent custom instruments: 100
Types of guitars built: Steel-string flat-tops, specialty guitars

Gruen Acoustic Guitars
PO Box 67766
Los Angeles, CA 90067
Phone: (323) 650-9155
Fax: (323) 650-9350

GUERNSEY RESOPHONIC GUITARS

Ivan Guernsey has played lap-style resonator guitar since 1971. In the mid-'80s Guernsey started researching the construction of resonator guitars, experimenting with various woods and their tonal properties, strategic bracing patterns, directional baffling systems, spider bridge inserts, resonator cones, and body designs. After completing this research and reading an interview with John Dopyera (the inventor of the resonator guitar), Guernsey decided that the body should be constructed of plywood for its strength and durability, resistance to cracks, and consistency of tap tone. In 1989, Guernsey built his first Regal-style resonator guitar, and this 1930s design is still in his line. In 1995, after three years of development, Guernsey added a modernized 800 series design to the lineup. These models are available in six- and eight-string versions. Standard features for all models include a square, mahogany neck joined to the body at the 12th fret; an ebony fingerboard; highly figured birch ply; high-quality 14:1 tuning machines; a Quarterman cone, and a deep, lacquer finish. Guernsey has built guitars for Mike Auldridge, Jerry Douglas, Vince Gill, Jim Heffernan, Stacy Phillips, and many other pickers.

First year of production: 1989
Approximate annual production: 25
Percent custom instruments: 70
Types of guitars built: Resonator guitars
Primary output: Lap-style resophonics
Custom options: Tuners, inlays, plating, finishes, pickups

Guernsey Resophonic Guitars
18402 Hwy 62
Marysville, IN 47141-9758
Phone: (812) 293-4524

GUILD GUITARS

Guild opened its custom shop in Nashville, Tennessee, in 1997 to raise public awareness of the company's tradition of fine craftsmanship, serve the needs of Guild players, and function as an R&D center for new Guild models. The custom shop's talented staff of craftsmen (headed by Bruce J. Bolen and including Tim Shaw, Mark Kendrick, Evan Ellis, and Mark Piper) is made up of some of the most experienced guitar builders in the world. Since its inception, the custom shop has been designing and crafting custom one-off acoustic guitars featuring superlative workmanship. The custom shop created a unique flattop for the Disney Store chain celebrating the Disney movie *Fantasia 2000.* It also introduced historic models designed by revered archtop builder Robert Benedetto, including the La Venezia,

which is played by jazz guitar virtuosos Frank Vignola, Ron Escheté, Howard Alden, and Bucky Pizzarelli.

First year of production: 1953
Approximate annual production: 12,000
Percent custom instruments: 2
Types of guitars built: Steel-string flattops, 12-strings, nylon-strings
Primary output: Steel-string flattops
Custom options: Finish, electronics, structure
Guitar pictured: p. 14

Guild Guitars
7975 Hayden Rd. #C-100
Scottsdale, AZ 85258-3246
Phone: (480) 596-7195
Fax: (480) 596-1386
www.guildguitars.com

HENNER HAGENLOCHER

Henner Hagenlocher served a six-month apprenticeship with Hamburg luthier Michael Wilson in 1986. He also attended the London Guildhall University, where he focused on classical guitar construction and experimented with computer analysis of sound. He has been building nylon-string and archtop guitars in Granada, Spain, since 1992.

First year of production: 1992
Approximate annual production: 15
Percent custom instruments: 100
Primary output: Nylon-strings
Custom options: Scale length, materials, bracing, tuners, rosettes

Henner Hagenlocher
Calle Guadarrama No. 3
Granada 8009
Spain
Phone: (34) 958-227966
Fax: (34) 958-137530

HANK TO HENDRIX GUITARS

Royden Moran has been building acoustic and electric guitars since 1996 when he took Bryan Galloup's guitar construction and repair course in Big Rapids, Michigan. That endeavor changed the course of his professional career (he had been an architect for 20 years). He returned to Peterborough, Ontario, and started the Hank to Hendrix guitar company with his friend Wayne O'Connor. The business occupies a 900-square-foot shop with a spray booth in a funky, old warehouse. Hank to Hendrix offers a complete range of professional repair services as well as custom-built acoustic and electric guitars. The design of Moran's acoustic guitar is based on the Gibson J-185 and is excellent for fingerpicking, flatpicking, and recording. His guitars are comfortable to play in a seated position. His Vintage series guitars feature a nitrocellulose lacquer finish and are available in figured maple, East Indian rosewood, and mahogany. Moran is

planning to expand his range of models to include a new instrument based on the Gibson L-1.

First year of production: 1996
Approximate annual production: 3–4
Percent custom instruments: 100
Types of guitars built: Steel-string flattops
Primary output: J-185–style guitars
Custom options: Tonewoods, cutaways, neck profiles, custom artwork
Guitar pictured: p. 18

Hank to Hendrix Guitars
Unit 11, 200 Perry St.
Peterborough, ON K9H 2J4
Canada
Phone: (705) 740-0965
Fax: (705) 748-2930
www.hanktohendrix.on.ca

J.T. HARGREAVES BASSES AND GUITARS

Jay Hargreaves has been building instruments since the early '70s. He studied informally for two years with violin maker Arthur Lockhart in Port Angeles, Washington; for two years at the Northwest School of Instrument Design in Seattle, Washington, with instructor Anthony Huvard; and for ten years as an apprentice for Richard Schneider at the Lost Mountain Center for the Guitar in Sequim, Washington. He worked as a teaching assistant for several years at each of these schools and has exhibited his instruments at numerous handmade musical instrument shows. Hargreaves builds acoustic bass guitars, classical guitars, and steel-string guitars. All his instruments use the Kasha/Schneider bracing system, and they are all designed individually for the customer and built one at a time.

First year of production: 1995
Approximate annual production: 2
Percent custom instruments: 100
Types of guitars built: Steel-string flattops, nylon-strings, specialty guitars
Primary output: Acoustic basses
Custom options: Woods, left-handed, string length, fretless, electronics, colors

J.T. Hargreaves Basses and Guitars
20226 2nd Ave. South
Seattle, WA 98198
Phone: (206) 878-2612
www.jthbass.com

LOUIS HAYES GUITARS

Louis Hayes has been a craftsman all his life. He has engaged in wood and stone sculpting, painting, leather work, pottery, and rustic furniture building, to name just a few of his endeavors. Guitar building married two of his great passions: woodworking and music. After two years and four guitars, Hayes enrolled in the American School of Lutherie in 1995 in order to turn his passion into a profession. There he studied both classi-

cal and steel-string guitar construction with such creative builder/teachers as Frank Ford, Jeffrey Elliott, Dana Bourgeois, Hideo Kamimoto, Charles Fox, and Jeff Traugott. He has been building guitars professionally since 1992 and operates a one-man shop in Carbondale, Colorado, just down the road from Aspen.

First year of production: 1993
Approximate annual production: 8–10
Types of guitars built: Steel-string flattops, 12-strings, nylon-strings, specialty guitars
Primary output: Steel-string flattops
Guitar pictured: p. 50

Louis Hayes Guitars
19 N. 4th St.
Carbondale, CO 81623
Phone: (970) 963-7133
www.hayesguitars.com

MICHAEL HEMKEN

Michael Hemken has worked in wood since his childhood in Minnesota. He taught himself to repair instruments in the early 1970s and built his first instrument, a mandola, in 1976. It was followed by violins, flattop guitars, and archtop guitars. Today Hemken specializes in hand-carved archtop guitars. His basic model is available with a variety of soundhole styles and placements, which produce different tonal qualities to meet the requirements of the player. Ornamentation is limited to custom bindings. Hemken displayed his guitars at the 1999 Healdsburg Guitar Festival and is a member of the Guild of American Luthiers and the Northern California Association of Luthiers.

First year of production: 1993
Approximate annual production: 6–10
Percent custom instruments: 100
Types of guitars built: Archtops
Guitar pictured: p. 86

Michael Hemken
1121 Zygmunt Dr.
St. Helena, CA 94574
Phone: (707) 963-8256

DENNIS HILL GUITARS

Dennis Hill began his career in guitars as a student of classical guitar teacher Ernesto Disk. He met guitar maker Augustino LoPrinzi in 1987 and became his East Coast sales representative. He later studied guitar making with LoPrinzi and moved to Panama City, Florida, to establish his own shop within Leitz Music in 1992. He builds classical, flamenco, steel-string, and archtop guitars, as well as concert violins, both at Leitz Music and in his private shop.

First year of production: 1991
Approximate annual production: 6 or more
Percent custom instruments: 20
Types of guitars built: Nylon-strings, archtops, specialty guitars

Primary output: Classicals and flamencos

Custom options: Wood choices

Guitar pictured: p. 71

Dennis Hill Guitars
508 Harrison Ave.
Panama City, FL 32401
Phone: (850) 769-3009

HILL GUITAR CO.

Kenny Hill divides his professional time between building handmade classical and flamenco guitars, performing, teaching guitar building, directing a guitar shop in Mexico, and writing for various national guitar magazines. He began building guitars in the mid-1970s, first in Santa Barbara, California, and later in the Santa Cruz area. In 1978 he was awarded one of the first California Arts Council grants for his work as a guitar builder and guitarist. From 1993 to 1995 he taught and directed an award-winning guitar-building program at Soledad State Prison, and he continues to teach inmates within the California State Prison System. In the late '90s, Hill's activities took on a more international trend and included work with some of Mexico's finest luthiers. He has helped raise the standard for a new generation of guitars being exported to the U.S. and other parts of the world. Hill is an active member of the GFA, GAL, ASIA, and NAMM and has participated in each association's expositions. Players of Kenny Hill guitars include Strunz and Farah, Tommy Jones, Donny Fontowitz, Chris Carnes, Earl Klugh, Teja Bell, and Stanley Yates.

First year of production: 1972

Approximate annual production: 225

Percent custom instruments: 10

Types of guitars built: Nylon-strings

Primary output: Classicals and flamencos

Custom options: Woods, string lengths, cutaways

Guitar pictured: p. 64

Hill Guitar Co.
501 Maple Ave.
Ben Lomond, CA 95006
Phone: (831) 336-2436
Fax: (831) 336-2436
www.hillguitar.com

HOFFMAN GUITARS

Charles Hoffman made his first guitar in 1970 and has since completed and sold nearly 400 steel-string acoustic guitars. Over the years he has built guitars for a number of nationally known performers, including Leo Kottke, Norman Blake, Dakota Dave Hull, and Ann Reed. He offers four body shapes: a dreadnought shape similar to the Martin dreadnought, a modified dreadnought patterned after the (14-fret) Gibson "slope-shoulder," a concert guitar (in 12- and 14-fret

versions) designed primarily for fingerpickers, and a 12-fret parlor guitar. He recently began building harp guitars as well. Each of his guitars is available in a wide variety of woods, and clients can choose from many custom options, including cutaways. Hoffman delights in working with his customers to create instruments that project their musical vision, in both sound and appearance. In addition to building guitars, Hoffman also runs the largest repair shop in the Midwest, providing warranty work for Martin, Taylor, Gibson, Fender, Guild, Olson, and other manufacturers.

First year of production: 1971

Approximate annual production: 8–12

Percent custom instruments: 100

Types of guitars built: Steel-string flattops, 12-strings, specialty guitars

Primary output: Steel-string flattops

Custom options: Cutaways, neck shapes, body shapes, inlay, carved heel, finish

Hoffman Guitars
2219 E. Franklin Ave.
Minneapolis, MN 55404
Phone/fax: (612) 338-1079
www.hoffmanguitars.com

HOLLENBECK GUITARS

As a teenager in central Illinois, Bill Hollenbeck was already a guitar aficionado. While other members of his family played piano, organ, and saxophone, Hollenbeck was busy adapting or embellishing his guitars. After attaining a B.A. in industrial arts and an M.A. in industry and technology, Hollenbeck embarked on a career in education, teaching electronics to high school students for 25 years. In 1970 he met Midwest luthier Bill Barker and began to serve as his apprentice, driving to Barker's shop on weekends for many years. In 1990 he left education to devote his career to full-time archtop guitar building, restoration, and repair. He now builds acoustic archtops in 16-, 17-, and 18-inch models as well as semi-hollow electric archtops. His instruments are known for their midrange attack, stability, and projection. Each guitar is customized for the player with the neck and fretboard fitted to the buyer's hands.

First year of production: 1970

Approximate annual production: 6

Percent custom instruments: 80–100

Types of guitars built: Archtops

Custom options: Body size, neck size, scale, thickness, colors, woods, inlay

Guitar pictured: p. 81

Hollenbeck Guitars
160 Half Moon St.
Lincoln, IL 62656
Phone: (217) 732-6933
www.hollenbeckguitar.com

THOMAS HUMPHREY

Thomas Humphrey started building

guitars in 1970 and developed his revolutionary Millennium model classical guitar in 1985. He has built Millenniums for many of the world's best classical players, including Sérgio and Odair Assad, Eliot Fisk, Sharon Isbin, Carlos Barbosa-Lima, and Michael Chapdelaine.

First year of production: 1970

Approximate annual production: 21

Percent custom instruments: 100

Types of guitars built: Nylon-strings

Custom options: None

Guitar pictured: p. 65

Thomas Humphrey
1167 Bruynswick Rd.
Gardiner, NY 12525
Phone/fax: (914) 256-0035
www.humphrey-guitars.com

HUSS AND DALTON GUITAR CO.

Jeff Huss and Mark Dalton began building instruments as employees of Stelling Banjo Works. After leaving Stelling, they teamed up to produce guitars. They now produce about 130 guitars per year with a five-man crew that includes John Calkin, a luthier with 20 years of experience. They also produce the Stelling guitar, which Jeff Huss designed while working for Stelling. About half of Huss and Dalton's instruments are standard models (there are nine models) and half are custom work. Their instruments are sold exclusively through a network of dealers.

First year of production: 1995

Approximate annual production: 130

Percent custom instruments: 50

Types of guitars built: Steel-string flattops

Custom options: Woods, bindings, purflings, inlays, neck sizes/shapes, sunbursts, 12-frets, scale length, etc.

Guitar pictured: p. 37

Huss and Dalton Guitar Co.
420 Bridge St.
Staunton, VA 24401
Phone: (540) 887-2313
Fax: (540) 887-2383
www.hussanddalton.com

JANOFSKY GUITARS

Stephen Janofsky studied guitar building with Earthworks in Vermont in 1977 and began building guitars part-time in 1978. He moved his shop from New York to Massachusetts in 1992 and has been building classical and flamenco guitars full-time ever since.

First year of production: 1980

Approximate annual production: 10

Percent custom instruments: 0

Types of guitars built: Nylon-strings

Primary output: Classicals and flamencos

Janofsky Guitars
493 West Pelham Rd.
Amherst, MA 01002
Phone: (413) 259-1072

JOHNSON GUITARS

David Lee Johnson began building guitars as a hobby in 1981 and became a full-time luthier in 1995. His shop was originally located in Alaska but recently moved to Campton, a small community in central New Hampshire. Johnson's flattop and archtop guitars are simple and elegant, built with high-quality materials and minimal ornamentation. When he's not building instruments, Johnson teaches students how to build flattop guitars in a one-on-one, two-week course.

First year of production: 1994

Approximate annual production: 25–30

Percent custom instruments: 20

Types of guitars built: Steel-string flattops, 12-strings, nylon-strings

Primary output: Steel-string flattops

Custom options: Woods, neck widths, cutaways, design

Johnson Guitars
17 Mountain View Rd.
Campton, NH 03223
Phone: (603) 726-0097
Fax: (603) 726-2008

JORDAN MUSIC SERVICES

John Jordan began his guitar-making career as an apprentice for Ervin Somogyi in 1980. He specializes in instruments built to order and has a way of helping customers articulate their dreams. Customers may choose the body shape, woods, bindings, purflings, inlays, and neck dimensions. His work has been profiled in the *New York Times, Musical Merchandise Review,* and *Frets.*

First year of production: 1980

Approximate annual production: 10

Percent custom instruments: 100

Types of guitars built: Steel-string flattops, 12-strings, nylon-strings, archtops, specialty guitars

Guitar pictured: p. 73

Jordan Music Services
1173 Linden Dr.
Concord, CA 94520
Phone: (925) 671-9246
Fax: (925) 687-6797
www.jordanmusic.com

STEPHEN KAKOS

Stephen Kakos built his first guitar in 1972 with the aid of Irving Sloane's book *Classic Guitar Construction.* He much preferred building guitars to learning to play them and sold his first instrument a few years later. He has been building and repairing traditional classical guitars ever since. His work is inspired by the guitars of Hauser, Santos, Esteso, Ramírez, Friedrich, Romanillos, and Rodriguez. Kakos' business is a one-man operation. He does all the work himself. He is happy to work with all of his customers to meet their needs.

First year of production: 1975

Approximate annual production: 12

Percent custom instruments: 20
Types of guitars built: Nylon-strings, specialty guitars
Primary output: Classicals
Custom options: Eight strings, cutaways, string length, pitch ranges

Stephen Kakos
1720 Finch Ln.
Mound, MN 55364
Phone: (952) 472-4732

KELLER GUITARS

As a guitarist with a deep love for the acoustic guitar, Michael L. Keller began building in 1975 under the guidance of Jeffrey Elliott. He became immersed in the hyperactive lutherie scene in Portland, Oregon, in 1976 and got to meet many master guitar builders, including Richard Schneider, Jimmy D'Aquisto, Michael Gurian, and Robert Lundberg. The impact of these makers on his career was enormous in that they exposed him to the highest level of guitar craftsmanship. His focus as a builder has been to create guitars that players really enjoy. His approach is fluid and experimental, and his instruments have constantly evolved. He strives to build six-string guitars that are brilliant in tone, rich in sustain and overtones, and fun to play. He offers everything from a massive, 18-inch jumbo guitar to a half-size baby guitar. All instruments are available with a full range of custom options.
First year of production: 1975
Approximate annual production: 12–16
Percent custom instruments: 50
Types of guitars built: Steel-string flattops, 12-strings, nylon-strings, archtops, Hawaiian guitars, specialty guitars
Custom options: Inlays, woods, fossil ivory nut, saddle, and bridge pins, neck width, scale
Guitar pictured: p. 46

Keller Guitars
2207 30th Ave. S.E.
Rochester, MN 55904
Phone: (507) 288-9226

KLEIN ACOUSTIC GUITARS

Steve Klein is dedicated to pushing the evolution of acoustic and electric guitar design. Over the years he has had the privilege and pleasure of meeting and working with great thinkers like Dr. Michael Kasha and Richard Schneider and great musicians, including Joe Walsh, Stephen Stills, Joni Mitchell, and David Lindley. In the '80s, inspired by friends Carl Margolis, Ronnie Montrose, and Neil Steinberger, he designed and built electric guitars for Bill Frisell, Lou Reed, David Torn, and Michael Hedges. He has built acoustic guitars for Andy Summers, Steve Miller, Joe Walsh, and Paul Schmidt. Klein

guitars are currently built by Steven Kauffman, an inspired woodworker who began building steel-string guitars in 1976. Klein and Kauffman have been working together since the late '80s.
First year of production: 1972
Approximate annual production: 14–18
Percent custom instruments: 50
Types of guitars built: Steel-string flattops, 12-strings, specialty guitars
Primary output: Kasha-inspired steel-strings
Custom options: Woods, neck widths, inlays
Guitar pictured: p. 36

Klein Acoustic Guitars
2560 Knob Hill Rd.
Sonoma, CA 95476
Phone/fax: (707) 938-4639
www.kleinguitars.com

KNUTSON LUTHIERY

John Knutson began playing and tinkering with guitars in the mid-'60s. He built his first Songbird archtop mandolin and dulcimer as school projects and has been a full-time luthier and repairman ever since. Knutson Luthiery was founded in 1981. As a custom builder of acoustic, archtop, and electric instruments, Knutson has produced hundreds of guitars, mandolins, dulcimers, and basses, including custom double- and triple-neck combinations. He has honed his production, research, and development skills by subcontracting for three larger companies out of his shop. He also does custom inlay work and builds the Messenger upright electric bass. Knutson is committed to being a one-man operation producing custom and limited-edition fine handmade instruments. Owners of his instruments include Lief Sorbye, David Lindley, Mike Marshall, and Mario Cippolina.
First year of production: 1981
Approximate annual production: 6
Percent custom instruments: 100
Types of guitars built: Steel-string flattops, archtops
Primary output: Archtops
Custom options: Inlays, woods, scale lengths

Knutson Luthiery
6812 Covey Rd.
Forrestville, CA 95436
Phone: (707) 887-2709
www.messengerbass.com

WILLIAM KRAMER-HARRISON

William Kramer-Harrison started his relationship with musical instruments as a collector and then apprenticed in the shop of Augustino LoPrinzi, where he was involved in the birth of LoPrinzi Guitars. After a year, Kramer-Harrison opened a small shop in New Hope, Pennsylvania, with partner Roger Sadowsky. In 1977 he moved to

Woodstock, New York, where he established a studio in the basement of Big Pink. There he ran a repair and restoration business for the local (but world-renowned) music community. Kramer-Harrison moved in 1984 to Kingston, New York, where he builds one-of-a-kind acoustic and classic guitars using traditional European methods, domestic and imported woods, and a French-polish finish.
First year of production: 1977
Approximate annual production: 5–10
Percent custom instruments: 100
Types of guitars built: Steel-string flattops, nylon-strings, specialty guitars
Primary output: Classicals

William Kramer-Harrison
302 Wall St.
Kingston, NY 12401
Phone: (914) 331-4145
Fax: (914) 340-4402

DOUG KYLE

D.A. Kyle is a guitar maker with a lifelong passion for guitar music and also an amateur jazz and blues player. He built his first guitar in 1975 and attended Norman Reed's guitar-making school in 1989. He repaired instruments while developing his own versions of archtop and Maccaferri-style guitars. He met and was asked to build guitars for some of the finest Gypsy players in Europe and has been busy ever since. He also builds and repairs double basses and violins, which influence and inform his guitar making.
First year of production: 1990
Approximate annual production: 12–15
Percent custom instruments: 100
Types of guitars built: Steel-string flattops, archtops
Primary output: Jazz guitars
Custom options: Scale length, fingerboard width, pickups

Doug Kyle
Fursdon, Moreton Hampstead
Devon TQ13 8QT
England
Phone: (44) 1647-440394
Fax: (44) 1647-440656

MARK LACEY GUITARS

Mark Lacey's career in building musical instruments began in 1974 when he attended the London College of Furniture and Interior Design, where he studied musical instrument technology. In 1977 he moved to Oslo, Norway, and spent the next four years working as a repairman for Norsk, Norway's largest importer of musical instruments. He moved to Nashville in 1981 to work as a repairman for vintage expert and dealer George Gruhn, where he was exposed to older archtop and flattop guitars. He relocated to Los Angeles in 1983 to run a custom guitar shop for pickup designer Bill Lawrence and later worked at the Guild guitar factory. He returned to

Los Angeles and started his own custom guitar and repair shop, the Guitar Garage, in 1988. He now concentrates on making archtop guitars in Nashville. Lacey's main influences have been John D'Angelico, Jimmy D'Aquisto, and Gibson, and his designs are fairly traditional. He bends the sides by hand, carves the tops and backs, and does his own inlay work. He usually builds between four and six instruments at a time and sets up each instrument according to the customer's specifications.
First year of production: 1974
Approximate annual production: 12–15
Percent custom instruments: 100
Types of guitars built: Steel-string flattops, 12-strings, archtops
Custom options: Inlays, tailpieces, neck sizes, woods
Guitar pictured: p. 75

Mark Lacey Guitars
PO Box 24646
Nashville, TN 37202
Phone: (615) 952-3045
Fax: (615) 952-4626
www.laceyguitars.com

LANGEJANS GUITARS

Born in Holland, Michigan, Delwyn J. Langejans was raised in a Christian family with a musical upbringing and a strong work ethic. He plays accordion and guitar and repaired electronics and band instruments at Meyer Music before opening Del's Guitar Gallery in 1970 (the name later changed to Del's Music Center). There he began building guitars and specializing in custom, handmade stringed instruments. He has built more than 1,000 instruments.
First year of production: 1971
Approximate annual production: 50–60
Percent custom instruments: 25
Types of guitars built: Steel-string flattops, 12-strings, nylon-strings
Custom options: Cutaways, abalone purfling, inlays, pickups, size variations
Guitar pictured: p. 25

Langejans Guitars
23 E. Eighth St.
Holland, MI 49423
Phone: (616) 396-4597
Fax: (616) 396-4598
www.langejansguitars.com

LARRIVEE GUITARS

Jean Larrivée met German luthier Edgar Münch while studying classical guitar in Toronto and built two guitars under Münch's tutelage before setting up a workshop in his home. He built strictly classical guitars—using his own distinctive shape, bracing patterns, and structural specifications—until 1971, when local folk musicians encouraged him to build steel-strings. Larrivée's steel-strings were classically inspired, with wood binding, marquetry rosettes, clear pickguards, and Renaissance-style inlays (designed and engraved by Jean's wife Wendy). The company grew steadily over the years, moving again and again to ever larger spaces. There was a continuous flow of apprentices through the shop, many of whom would go on to become successful builders in their own right. Larrivée designed and built specialized machines and tooling that allowed him to produce high-quality instruments in larger quantities and got involved for a time in building solid-body electric guitars in the 1980s. Larrivée's 100 highly skilled employees build 60 guitars a day, using a combination of old-world crafts-manship and modern technology.

First year of production: 1967
Approximate annual production: 9,000
Percent custom instruments: 2
Types of guitars built: Steel-string flat-tops, 12-strings, nylon-strings, spe-cialty guitars
Primary output: Steel-string flattops
Guitar pictured: p. 40

Larrivée Guitars
780 E. Cordova St.
Vancouver, BC V6A 1M3
Canada
Phone: (604) 253-7111
Fax: (604) 253-5447
www.larrivee.com

LASKIN GUITARS

William "Grit" Laskin wears many hats. His primary one is that of a gui-tar maker, a profession he has pur-sued since 1970. His steel-string, clas-sical, and flamenco guitars are known and coveted around the world. Players of his instruments include kd lang, Ben Mink, Rik Emmett, Tom Cochrane, Jesse Cook, Wayne Johnson, Tom Chapin, and Ottmar Liebert. In addition to building the instruments, Laskin uses them as "canvases" for his engraved inlay art. To encourage the growth and public awareness of the luthier's craft, Laskin cofounded in 1988 (and twice was president of) the Association of Stringed Instrument Artisans (ASIA), the international trade organization geared to profes-sional builders and repairers of musi-cal instruments. He has also been a multi-instrumental performer of music, playing guitar, mandolin, Northumbrian smallpipes, and con-certina. He continues to concertize in clubs and music festivals across Canada and the northern U.S. and has recorded four solo albums of original music. He also cofounded Borealis Records, Canada's first national folk music label, in 1996; is one of the coordinators of the Woods Music and Dance Camp; and has published two books.

First year of production: 1973
Approximate annual production: 12–14

Percent custom instruments: 100
Types of guitars built: Steel-string flat-tops, 12-strings, nylon-strings, specialty guitars
Custom options: Inlays, alternative woods, ergonomic designs
Guitar pictured: p. 48

Laskin Guitars
26 Noble St. #12
Toronto, ON M6K 2C9
Canada
Phone: (416) 536-2135
Fax: (416) 533-8705

H.G. LEACH GUITARS

Harvey Leach began his career as a luthier by building a banjo from the wood of a maple tree he chopped down in his parents' backyard in 1973. Since 1988 he has concentrated on acoustic guitars—both flattops and archtops—though he has added hol-low-body and solid-body electrics to his line. Located in the Sierra Nevada foothills of northern California, Leach produces about 20 high-end custom instruments per year. Inlays are his hallmark, and he specializes in theme guitars where inlay patterns, carvings, and construction materials are care-fully selected and artfully blended together. He works one-on-one with his customers, matching wood choic-es and aesthetics with each individ-ual's playing style, needs, and dreams. For Leach there is no greater satisfac-tion than meeting the challenge of a player's specific needs.

First year of production: 1980
Approximate annual production: 25–30
Percent custom instruments: 100
Types of guitars built: Steel-string flat-tops, 12-strings, nylon-strings, arch-tops, specialty guitars
Primary output: Steel-string flattops
Custom options: Inlays, neck carvings, scrimshaw, engraving, etc.
Guitar pictured: p. 21

H.G. Leach Guitars
PO Box 1315
Cedar Ridge, CA 95924
Phone: (530) 477-2938
www.leachguitars.com

JOHN LE VOI GUITARS

John Le Voi began making guitars pro-fessionally in 1970. He fell in love with the Gypsy jazz style of Django Reinhardt and the Quintet of the Hot Club of France and was asked to restore a D-hole Maccaferri guitar in 1976. He became fascinated with Maccaferri guitars and began making reproductions of the D-hole model and later of the Selmer-type guitar with the small oval soundhole. As the years have passed, he has modified the original designs only slightly. The guitars retain the original dimensions, scale length, and belly arch. Le Voi has changed the bracing pattern where the originals have shown signs of dis-

tress, but he is happy to build exact replicas upon request. He works alone, which limits his production totals but allows him to incorporate customers' individual requests.

First year of production: 1970
Approximate annual production: 20
Percent custom instruments: 50
Types of guitars built: Steel-string flat-tops, 12-strings, nylon-strings, arch-tops, specialty guitars
Primary output: Maccaferri-style guitars
Custom options: Woods, shapes, etc.
Guitar pictured: p. 105

John Le Voi Guitars
The Workshop
West St.
Alford, Lincs LN13 9EZ
England
Phone: (44) 1507-463341
www.levoi.freeserve.co.uk

MICHAEL LEWIS INSTRUMENTS

Michael Lewis has been a professional repairman since 1981, the year that he began building mandolins. As a result of his experience carving mandolins, he was invited to join D'Angelico Guitars in 1993, where he helped to create some of the finest archtop gui-tars ever made. At the same time he began building dreadnoughts for bluegrass musicians as well as small-er-bodied and Hawaiian guitars. He spends more than 80 percent of his time in the shop making instruments and less than 20 percent doing repair work. He enjoys re-creating traditional designs, but he prefers to develop and incorporate new ideas and designs. He says that he "colors inside the lines, but reserves the right to move the lines."

First year of production: 1992
Approximate annual production: 12
Percent custom instruments: 100
Types of guitars built: Steel-string flat-tops, archtops, Hawaiian guitars
Primary output: Archtops, mandolins
Custom options: Materials, trim, col-ors, inlays, neck profile, pickups
Guitar pictured: p. 73

Michael Lewis Instruments
20807 E. Spring Ranches Rd.
Grass Valley, CA 95949
Phone: (530) 272-4124
www.svlg.org

JEREMY LOCKE GUITARS

Jeremy Locke began building instru-ments in the early 1980s, while he was studying classical guitar with Jason Waldron in Adelaide, Australia. He travels the world to visit other luthiers, purchase materials, and improve his craft. He has exhibited guitars at the Healdsburg Guitar Festival and the annual meeting of the Guitar Foundation of America, where a player using one of his instruments

won first prize at the 1999 competi-tion in Charleston. He primarily builds classical and flamenco guitars, using exotic species of timber, as well as the odd steel-string acoustic.

First year of production: 1985
Approximate annual production: 20
Percent custom instruments: 25
Types of guitars built: Nylon-strings
Custom options: Rosettes, scale, fret-board width, cutaways, left-handed, inlays, pickups, finishes, woods

Jeremy Locke Guitars
90 Finnegan Way
Coomera, QLD
Australia
Phone/fax: (61) 7-55299738
www.classicalandflamencoguitars.com

ABEL GARCIA LOPEZ

Abel Garcia Lopez was born in Paracho, the center of guitar construc-tion in Mexico. His family has been making guitars for five generations. In 1992 he was awarded a scholarship from the Mexican National Arts Council to participate at the Festival de Cordoba with J. Luis Romanillos, Leo Brouwer, and Angelo Gilardino, among others. He has since founded his own course on guitar construction at the University of Michoacan. He has also lectured in universities throughout Mexico as well as in the U.S. His instruments are played by Pepe and Celedonio Romero, Miguel Angel Lejarza, Alfonso Moreno, Antonio Lopez, Andrew Schulman, and Gerard Edery. Lopez is also a leading expert in the restoration of period instruments and the author of two books on guitars.

First year of production: 1985
Approximate annual production: 12–15
Percent custom instruments: 100
Types of guitars built: Nylon-strings, specialty guitars
Primary output: classicals

Abel Garcia Lopez
Guerrero 383
Paracho, Michoacan 60250
Mexico
Phone: (452) 5-02-39
Fax: (452) 5-08-73

LUCAS CUSTOM INSTRUMENTS

Randy Lucas began his career in lutherie in 1988 when he took a part-time job as a repairman at a local music store. In 1990 he converted his one-car garage into a workshop, where he began studying, repairing, and restoring vintage acoustic Martin and Gibson guitars and mandolins. By 1993 his love for vintage guitars led him to build a handful of traditional guitars, and he decided to make guitar building a full-time occupation soon thereafter. In 1997 he built a 1,500-square-foot, climate-controlled work-shop in order to meet the ever-increasing demand for new Lucas guitars. His lineup includes dreadnoughts, OMs, and jumbos, and he offers a wide range of options, including various inlays and wood species. Until recently, most of his guitars were built using traditional body shapes and peghead outlines, but Lucas is in the process of adding a new line of guitar models that will incorporate his own designs and body shapes. He also has plans to build classical guitars and mandolins.

First year of production: 1989
Approximate annual production: 12–15
Percent custom instruments: 50
Types of guitars built: Steel-string flattops

Lucas Custom Instruments
PO Box 1404
Columbus, IN 7202
Phone: (812) 342-3093
www.lucasguitars.com

S.B. MACDONALD CUSTOM GUITARS

Scott MacDonald started building guitars in 1980 and turned his hobby into a career at the age of 30. He is a member of ASIA and writes a column in *20th-Century Guitar* magazine. He strives to create instruments as unique as the people who play them. He shapes the sound and design around the customer's physical requirements and vocal tone. He also taught guitar making at a college for several years until his business required his full attention. He is now building at an international level and having a great time!

First year of production: 1988
Approximate annual production: 20–30
Percent custom instruments: 100
Types of guitars built: Steel-string flattops, 12-srings, resonator guitars, specialty guitars
Guitar pictured: p. 20

S.B. MacDonald Custom Guitars
22 Fairmont St.
Huntington, NY 11743-3502
Phone/fax: (631) 421-9056
www.customguitars.com

DAVE MAIZE ACOUSTIC GUITARS

Dave Maize's earliest training in lutherie came in 1975, when he took a guitar-making class from Mark Platin of Wildwood Banjos in Arcata, California. With a meager supply of skills and tools, he made a guitar that is actually still playable. For the next several years he pursued other interests and then returned to lutherie in 1990. In a small shop in Oregon's Rogue River Valley, he now builds acoustic guitars and basses using a combination of SmartWood forest-certified woods and SmartWood rediscovered woods (reclaimed from sources such as demolition projects and trees that needed to be cut). The origin of the materials he uses and the way in which they were harvested are just as important to Maize as their appearance and tonal properties. His instruments are available from the shop where he builds about ten per year and are played by such musicians as Adam Clayton (U2), Phil Lesh (Grateful Dead), Jack Casady (Hot Tuna), and Jeff Ament (Pearl Jam). In addition to guitars, he offers a wide variety of guitar woods, most of which are certified by SmartWood.

First year of production: 1991
Approximate annual production: 10
Percent custom instruments: 50
Types of guitars built: Steel-string flattops, specialty guitars
Custom options: Certified SmartWood, cutaways, neck width
Guitar pictured: p. 37

Dave Maize Acoustic Guitars
999 Holton Rd.
Talent, OR 97540
Phone: (888) 242-0846
www.maizeguitars.com

MANZANITA GUITARS

Manzanita Guitars was formed by Manfred Pietrzok and Moritz Sattler in 1993. Pietrzok started out in 1980 doing shellac and spirit-varnish finishes for all kinds of stringed instruments. He apprenticed with violin maker James Wimmer in Santa Barbara, California, off and on between 1985 and 1990 and then opened his own guitar-making business in 1992. He began by designing and building all kinds of slide instruments as well as flatpicking guitars but soon realized that he wasn't cut out to run a one-person assembly line. He now works only on special designs that are thoroughly customized for sound, appearance, and playability. Sattler attended the Mittenwald violin-making school (1982–85) and worked for several German manufacturers before opening his own workshop in 1991. At Manzanita Guitars, he focuses on fingerstyle flattops, replicas of prewar instruments, and nylon-string guitars for steel-string players.

First year of production: 1993
Approximate annual production: 16
Percent custom instruments: 100
Types of guitars built: Steel-string flattops, 12-strings, nylon-strings, resonator guitars, Hawaiian guitars, specialty guitars
Primary output: Resonators and Hawaiians
Guitar pictured: p. 89

Manzanita Guitars
Sellenfried 3
D-37124 Rosdorf
Germany
Phone/fax: (49) 551-782-417
www.manzanita.de

MANZER GUITARS

Linda Manzer graduated with honors from the Sheridan College of Art and Design in Toronto before apprenticing with Jean Larrivée from 1974 to 1978 and with James D'Aquisto in 1983. She is a member of ASIA and the GAL and has exhibited her guitars at numerous ASIA symposia as well as various museums and festivals in Canada. She currently lives in Toronto, where she builds instruments for a roster of players and collectors that includes Liona Boyd, Bruce Cockburn, Stephen Fearing, Gordon Lightfoot, Pat Metheny, and Carlos Santana.

First year of production: 1976
Approximate annual production: 15–20
Percent custom instruments: 100
Types of guitars built: Steel-string flattops, 12-strings, nylon-strings, archtops, specialty guitars
Custom options: Custom necks, scale, "wedge" design, inlays, etc.
Guitars pictured: pp. 62, 105

Manzer Guitars
65 Metcalfe St.
Toronto, ON M4X 1R9
Canada
Phone: (416) 927-1539
Fax: (416) 927-8233
www.manzer.com

MARCHIONE GUITARS

Steve Marchione builds recording-quality archtops and special commissions in his Manhattan shop. His clientele consists primarily of guitar lovers and players like Mark Whitfield, John Abercrombie, and Mark Knopfler. He approaches the craft from many different angles. He understands players' sound and comfort needs because he is a player himself. As a builder, he has studied great instruments in the guitar and violin traditions. Whenever a player brings a D'Aquisto or a D'Angelico to his shop, he scrutinizes the instrument's construction, draws plans, and asks the player about the instrument's best qualities. He then incorporates those elements into his own designs. A hands-on understanding of cello arching is fundamental to achieving the subtleties that imbue Marchione guitars with full acoustic volume and timbre. He has also studied violins, which have taught him how to build a truly acoustic archtop.

First year of production: 1993
Approximate annual production: 35
Percent custom instruments: 100
Types of guitars built: Nylon-strings, archtops, specialty guitars
Primary output: Archtops
Guitar pictured: p. 83

Marchione Guitars
20 W. 20th St., Suite 806
New York, NY 10011
Phone: (212) 675-5215
www.marchione.com

C.F. MARTIN AND CO.

C.F. Martin and Co., founded by Christian Frederick Martin Sr. in 1833, remains the oldest surviving maker of guitars in the world and the largest acoustic guitar maker in America. Martin guitars continue to be prized for their tone, consistency, quality, and attention to handcrafted detail. The list of Martin players past and present reads like a who's who of the musical world and includes legends such as Elvis Presley, Paul McCartney, Eric Clapton, Hank Williams Sr., Jimmy Buffett, Stephen Stills, Neil Young, and Joan Baez. Martin was one of the first companies to initiate a custom shop, where the discerning guitarist can design an instrument that is uniquely their own. From selection of tonewoods and trim to the size and shape of the neck, just about any combination of Martin body sizes, style appointments, and pearl inlay motifs are possible. In addition, quotations will be made on customized "conversion model upgrades" from older Martin instruments. In addition to guitar making, Martin is also one of the world's largest manufacturers of musical strings and a major distributor of fretted instrument accessories.

First year of production: 1833
Approximate annual production: 60,000
Percent custom instruments: 2
Types of guitars built: Steel-string flattops, 12-strings, nylon-strings
Primary output: Steel-string flattops
Guitars pictured: pp. 12, 47

C.F. Martin and Co.
510 Sycamore St.
Nazareth, PA 18064-1058
Phone: (610) 759-2837
Fax: (610) 759-5757
www.martinguitar.com

MAUEL GUITARS

Hank Mauel built his first guitar in 1972. After working for more than 20 years as a self-taught hobbyist luthier, he finally set up a professional shop in 1995. Located in the Sierra Foothills town of Auburn, California, the shop offers five standard steel-string models with a long list of options and alternative tonewoods. Variations to individual models and special design requests are easily accomplished. With a total production of about 24 instruments per year, each guitar receives the personal attention that maximizes its full potential of tone, volume, and sustain. Customers are encouraged to visit the shop, choose the woods and trimmings that will personalize their instrument, and enjoy a one-to-one relationship with Mauel as he builds their special guitar.

First year of production: 1995

Approximate annual production: 24–30
Percent custom instruments: 100
Types of guitars built: Steel-string flattops, 12-strings
Primary output: Steel-string flattops
Custom options: Woods, inlays, neck and fingerboard dimensions, scale lengths
Guitar pictured: p. 21

Mauel Guitars
PO Box 3014
Auburn, CA 95604
Phone: (503) 885-1265
www.svlg.org/member/mauel

McALISTER GUITARS

In 1973 Roy McAlister received his first guitar as a Christmas gift. Four years later he took a job at an antique restoration shop and immediately fell in love with everything about the shop. After working there for two months, he brought his guitar in for "a little customizing" and has been hooked ever since. He studied the craft of fine furniture design and construction and continued to build and customize guitars for himself and his friends on the side. He met Richard Hoover of the Santa Cruz Guitar Co. and went to work for him in 1992. He built guitars at SCGC for four years before leaving to start his own guitar-making shop. With 20 years of experience as a fine furniture builder and the knowledge gained during his years at SCGC, he began building guitars under his own name, attracting such customers as Jackson Browne, David Crosby, and Graham Nash.

First year of production: 1997
Approximate annual production: 18–20
Percent custom instruments: 100
Types of guitars built: Steel-string flattops, 12-strings, specialty guitars
Primary output: Steel-string flattops
Guitar pictured: p. 44

McAlister Guitars
40 Eucalyptus Dr.
Watsonville, CA 95076
Phone: (831) 761-2519
www.mcalisterguitars.com

McCOLLUM GUITARS

Lance McCollum began building handmade guitars because he simply couldn't find the sound he was looking for in guitars he could buy off the rack. McCollum began gathering the skills he would need as a guitar maker early in life. At the age of 12 he redesigned a couple of BMX bicycles, welding the new forms together and embellishing them with fancy paint jobs. In his teenage years he began designing and shaping his own surfboards, reconfiguring the fin placement and topping them off with airbrushed artwork. In high school he won awards in drafting class and developed an affinity for making jewelry. The first guitar he built was from

a modified Martin kit, and he has now been building full-time since 1994. His instruments are played by Alex de Grassi, Richard Leo Johnson, Dougie MacLean, and Doug Smith, among many others.

First year of production: 1995
Approximate annual production: 40
Percent custom instruments: 100
Types of guitars built: Steel-string flattops, 12-strings, specialty guitars
Primary output: Steel-string flattops
Guitar pictured: p. 31

McCollum Guitars
PO Box 806
Colfax, CA 95713
Phone: (530) 346-7657
Fax: (530) 346-7357
www.mccollumguitars.com

McCURDY GUITARS

Archtop guitar maker Ric McCurdy built his first instrument—a bass guitar—in his apartment with hand tools. It sounded better than his commercial bass. He later met Santa Barbara–area repairman John Hawk, who hired him to do repairs. Hawk had studied at the Bozo School of Luthiery in San Diego. After several months under Hawk's tutelage, McCurdy had the opportunity to work for Phil Kubicki. He opened his own repair shop in 1983 and developed a reputation for being able to build anything: eight-string bouzoukis, double-neck basses, fretless guitars, and archtops with two bass strings and four guitar strings. In January 1993 he took Bob Benedetto's incredibly informative archtop-building class. He had already built an archtop, but Benedetto showed him how to tap-tune the plates to get the "big, D'Angelico-type sound." McCurdy was hooked on archtop guitars and stopped doing repair work in 1999 to work exclusively on his backlog of archtop orders.

First year of production: 1983
Approximate annual production: 12–18
Percent custom instruments: 80
Types of guitars built: Steel-string flattops, nylon-strings, archtops, specialty guitars
Primary output: Archtops
Guitar pictured: p. 81

McCurdy Guitars
19 Hudson St.
New York, NY 10013
Phone/fax: (212) 274-8352
www.mccurdyguitars.com

McGILL GUITARS

Paul McGill's career began at the Earthworks School in Vermont, where he studied with well-respected luthier Charles Fox. By the late '70s McGill had made his way to Wisconsin, where he built and repaired instruments for local musicians, including Pat and Barbara MacDonald (Timbuk3) and Free Hot Lunch. In

1985 McGill moved to Nashville, Tennessee, to work in the Gruhn repair and restoration shop, where he remained until 1988. This experience allowed him to study vintage instruments, including D'Angelicos and pre-war Martins. He began building classical guitars for such players as Earl Klugh and Muriel Anderson and completed his first resonator guitar in 1992. His unique instruments have been featured on recordings by Chet Atkins, Ricky Skaggs, Phil Keaggy, and Steve Earle. In the late '90s McGill introduced the Super Ace acoustic-electric, which was inspired by the pickup design work of Richard McClish and redefines the practical parameters of acoustic-electric instruments. The Super Ace is played by contemporary jazz artists Peter White and Marc Antoine, among others.

First year of production: 1976
Approximate annual production: 20
Types of guitars built: Nylon-strings, resonator guitars
Primary output: Nylon-strings
Guitar pictured: p. 93

McGill Guitars
808 Kentall
Nashville, TN 37209
Phone: (615) 354-0070
Fax: (615) 352-9876
www.mcgillguitars.com

McPHERSON GUITARS

The McPherson Guitar Co. was started in 1981 by Mander McPherson, whose original model featured three sound-holes (Taj Mahal is still seen using them in performance). The company has now grown to be the largest archery company in the world as well as producing the new 777 model guitar, designed by McPherson's son Matt. It features unusual bracing patterns and new-age technology. McPherson guitars are played by Reba McEntire, Ricky Skaggs, Bob Carlisle, Phil Keaggy, and Jason Carter. The company produces approximately 40–60 instruments per year and hopes to begin selling them to the public in 2001.

First year of production: 1981
Approximate annual production: 40–60
Percent custom instruments: 0
Types of guitars built: Steel-string flattops
Guitar pictured: p. 19

McPherson Guitars
919 River Rd.
Sparta, WI 54656
Phone: (608) 269-2728
Fax: (608) 269-6770

MEGAS GUITARS

Ted Megas' skill at creating archtop guitars is the confluence of two guiding passions in his life: music and fine woodworking and metalworking. In the early '70s he led a double life as a custom furniture builder by day and a

guitarist by night. In the mid-'70s he began building guitars. He experimented with designs and concepts and finally focused his energies on the archtop guitar. Working alone in his San Francisco shop, Megas produces 12 custom instruments each year, handling every aspect of design and production from beginning to end. Megas' unique archtop guitars are owned by collectors and players around the world and are cherished for their singular design and construction.

First year of production: 1975
Approximate annual production: 12
Percent custom instruments: 100
Types of guitars built: Archtops
Custom options: Woods, inlays, appointments
Guitars pictured: pp. 79, 85

Megas Guitars
1070 Van Dyke
San Francisco, CA 94124
Phone: (415) 822-3100
Fax: (415) 822-1454
www.megasguitars.com

JOHN F. MELLO

During his four years at Oberlin College, John F. Mello enthusiastically built two fairly sloppy instruments. After graduation he apprenticed under Richard Schneider and later worked with Jeff Elliott. They taught Mello the standards and techniques that are the basis of his work today. Since 1972 he has built and restored guitars in his Bay Area shop. His work on instruments by most major makers of the last 150 years, including two Antonio de Torres guitars, has uniquely informed his own building. Mello favors light construction, fairly shallow bodies, and thin finishes. His steel-string guitars are loud and clear, with a strong bass, a broad selection of tonal colors, and a wide dynamic range. His classical guitars are more articulate and singing than they are big and punchy. The basses have a strong fundamental with good definition, and the trebles are clear and crystalline. Changes in dynamics, angle of attack, and hand position yield distinctly different sounds on a Mello guitar.

First year of production: 1973
Approximate annual production: 12–18
Percent custom instruments: 10
Types of guitars built: Steel-string flattops, 12-strings, nylon-strings
Custom options: Scale length, neck shape, purfling, woods
Guitar pictured: p. 45

John F. Mello
437 Colusa Ave.
Kensington, CA 94707
Phone: (510) 528-1080
www.johnfmello.com

MELVILLE GUITARS

Christopher Melville began playing the

guitar in the late 1970s and has been building and repairing acoustic guitars since 1988. He builds only a few instruments each year and spends most of his time doing repair work. Each guitar he makes exhibits great volume, balance, sweetness of tone, and sustain. His instruments feature traditional design and construction, and Melville pays close attention to details, such as wood selection, accurate fretwork, proper setup with precise intonation, and a slender and playable neck that resists twisting. These are just a few of the many details that result in a guitar that looks and sounds wonderful and also plays beautifully throughout its life.

First year of production: 1988
Approximate annual production: 5–8
Percent custom instruments: 100
Types of guitars built: Steel-string flattops, 12-strings
Primary output: Steel-string flattops
Guitar pictured: p. 47

Melville Guitars
PO Box 161
Kenmore
Brisbane, Queensland 4069
Australia
Phone: (61) 7-3878-7800
www.melvilleguitars.com

MENKEVICH GUITARS

The Menkevich classical guitar is truly state of the art. Menkevich carefully selects the materials for their acoustic and visual characteristics and then works to optimize their potential. His guitars feature graceful body shapes, a pronounced taper from the lower to the upper bout, and a fast and light neck set up with medium action and string spacing for playability. The voice is sustained, well balanced, and clear, with powerful projection. The tone colors that can be brought forth from a Menkevich guitar encompass the entire musical palette. The balance, look, and feel of the guitar combine to create a strong artistic impression. All Menkevich guitars are built in a climate-controlled environment and are guaranteed for the life of the original owner. They continue to improve with age.

First year of production: 1970
Approximate annual production: 20
Percent custom instruments: 30
Types of guitars built: Nylon-strings
Primary output: Classicals and flamencos

Menkevich Guitars
624 Stetson Rd.
Elkins Park, PA 19027
Phone: (215) 635-0694
www.menkevich.com

MERMER GUITARS

Richard Mermer has been designing, building, and repairing fretted stringed instruments since 1983. He studied guitar building at the Roberto-Venn School of Luthiery and acquired additional experience working for Fretted Instruments International and Philip Kubicki Guitar Technology. Mermer's shop is not geared toward mass production, although jigs and tooling are certainly used to cut down on the time spent on the more tedious and repetitious steps in the construction process. Generally Mermer builds one to three instruments at a time, handcrafting each of them to the specifications of the client and using the finest materials. Mermer guitars are used in the studio and in live performance by many artists, including Don Conoscenti, Cyril Pahinui, Brooks Williams, John Alevizakis, and Al Scortino. Mermer has been a member of both the Guild of American Luthiers and the Association of Stringed Instrument Artisans since 1983. He participated on a panel at ASIA Symposium '93, and his instruments have been featured in *Acoustic Guitar* and *Guitarmaker* magazines.

First year of production: 1983
Approximate annual production: 12–16
Percent custom instruments: 80
Types of guitars built: Steel-string flattops, 12-strings, nylon-strings, Hawaiian guitars, specialty guitars
Primary output: Steel-strings, Hawaiian guitars
Guitars pictured: pp. 46, 94

Mermer Guitars
PO Box 782132
Sebastian, FL 32978
Phone: (561) 388-0317
www.gate.net/~mermer

MERRILL GUITAR CO.

Jim Merrill began repairing guitars in the late 1970s and has had the opportunity to work on some of the finest acoustic instruments ever made. His own guitars have benefitted from the knowledge he gained from repair work, proving beyond a doubt that the early makers came up with great designs. His guitars differ slightly from the original designs in order to accommodate modern musicians who travel frequently through many climates and need instruments with adjustable necks. Merrill puts a part of himself into all the guitars he builds, from the very ornate archtops to the simplest Hauser-inspired classical guitars.

First year of production: 1998
Approximate annual production: 75
Percent custom instruments: 55
Types of guitars built: Steel-string flattops, nylon-strings, archtops, specialty guitars
Primary output: Steel-string flattops

Merrill Guitar Co.
140 B Tewning Rd.
Williamsburry, VA 23188
Phone: (757) 229-7966
www.merrillguitar.com

MINSTREL GUITARS

Minstrel guitar maker Bill Mitchell has been building and designing guitars since 1979. After attending the Timberline School of Lutherie, Mitchell became a full-time guitar maker in 1992, and he now operates a one-man building and repair shop in New Jersey.

First year of production: 1980
Approximate annual production: 20–30
Percent custom instruments: 50
Types of guitars built: Steel-string flattops, 12-strings
Primary output: Steel-string flattops
Custom options: Inlays, left-handed, cutaways, woods, neck profiles
Guitar pictured: p. 30

Minstrel Guitars
906 17th Ave.
Wall, NJ 07719
Phone: (732) 681-3430
www.minstrelguitars.com

ERIC MONRAD

Eric Monrad began repairing and building instruments in 1976. He builds and French-polishes classical and flamenco guitars in the Spanish manner and uses handmade marquetry rosettes and purfling. He offers spruce, cedar, and redwood soundboards and a range of tonewoods for backs and sides, including traditional redwoods, maple, cypress, and alternative woods. As a resident of Healdsburg, California, Monrad delights in his community's growing status as a center of lutherie. He has exhibited at the Healdsburg Guitar Festivals and is a member of the Guild of American Luthiers and the Northern California Association of Luthiers.

First year of production: 1993
Approximate annual production: 8–10
Percent custom instruments: 100
Types of guitars built: Nylon-strings
Primary output: Classicals and flamencos
Custom options: Woods, scale length, fingerboard width, neck profile
Guitar pictured: p. 54

Eric Monrad
7566 Eastside Rd.
Healdsburg, CA 95448
Phone: (707) 838-7823
Fax: (707) 838-7241

MONTELEONE GUITARS

Noted guitar builder John Monteleone strives to create a harmonic visual relationship among the various parts of his instruments that coincides with sound. He usually begins a guitar's design with the fretboard and body shape, taking into account such components as scale length, body size, and depth. His next consideration is the materials to be used in the instrument's construction. Each guitar is an individual based on its component parts and materials, and Monteleone makes all of the parts himself. Every aspect of construction is integral to the instrument's final outcome. Monteleone celebrated his 26th year as a luthier in 2000. He got his start in the business building mandolins and doing restoration and repair work for Mandolin Brothers in Staten Island, New York. Since then he has focused his attention on improving the sound and structural integrity of his guitars and mandolins. A recent advance is his trademarked Monteleone Side-Sound system, which allows the guitar to project forward to the audience and upward to the player. His design allows him to place a variety of side soundholes without jeopardizing the structural integrity of the top, sides, and back.

First year of production: 1975
Approximate annual production: 12–15
Percent custom instruments: 50
Types of guitars built: Steel-string flattops, archtops
Primary output: Archtops
Custom options: Monteleone side soundholes
Guitar pictured: p. 84

Monteleone Guitars
PO Box 52
Islip, NY 11751
Phone: (631) 277-3620
Fax: (631) 277-3639
www.monteleone.net

MOONSTONE GUITARS

Steve Helgeson of Moonstone Guitars has been producing some of the world's finest handcrafted acoustic, electric, and bass guitars since the early 1970s. From the beginning, he used highly figured and exotic tonewoods, pioneering the use of Pacific quilted maple, myrtlewood, maple, and walnut burl. His shop grew larger and larger in the late '70s and reached its peak production, 1,000 instruments per year, in the early '80s. After his shop was destroyed by fire, Helgeson began working alone to design and voice new acoustic guitars, personally carving and bracing all of his guitar tops, tap-tuning each one, and fine-tuning his operation. His instruments can be found in the hands of such players as Greg Allman, J.J. Cale, Henry Kaiser, and the Artist (Prince). Moonstone is pleased to custom-build any guitar to meet individual specifications.

First year of production: 1972
Approximate annual production: 15–20
Percent custom instruments: 50
Types of guitars built: Steel-string flattops, 12-strings, archtops, specialty guitars
Primary output: Flattops, electrics
Custom options: Woods, trim, inlays, bindings, finish, pickups, rosettes
Guitar pictured: p. 26

Moonstone Guitars
PO Box 757
Eureka, CA 95502
Phone: (707) 445-9045
www.northcoast.com/~moongtar

MORTORO GUITARS

Gary Mortoro began building archtop guitars in 1991 under the guidance of Robert Benedetto. Since he was a young boy his interest was always rooted in jazz, and playing the guitar was an integral part of his youth. He studied under Joe Cinderella and various other accomplished musicians. He learned woodworking from his father. Constructing guitars combines his love of jazz and his love of woodworking.

First year of production: 1992
Approximate annual production: 12–15
Percent custom instruments: 100
Types of guitars built: Archtops
Custom options: Body and neck dimensions, colors, inlays, multiple strings, pickups
Guitar pictured: p. 75

Mortoro Guitars
PO Box 161225
Miami, FL 33116-1225
Phone: (305) 238-7947
Fax: (305) 259-8745

DON MUSSER GUITARS

Don Musser was first exposed to fine craftsmanship while working in the shop of his father, Penrod Musser, a master gunsmith and machinist who makes replicas of early Colt firearms. In the 1970s he was drawn to lutherie through exposure to three L.A. guitar makers: Marc Whitebook, David Russell Young, and Roy Noble. He developed a deep appreciation for beautiful and scarce woods and materials while sharing a shop with Chuck "Duke of Pearl" Erikson in the 1980s. Over the years, Musser's guitars have been marketed primarily through Norman Harris at Norm's Rare Guitars in Reseda, California. His focus is on the limited production of six to ten instruments per year that highlight exceptionally high-quality materials and craftsmanship. His instruments are continuously evolving in terms of refinement of tone and playability. They are owned by such musicians as Tom Rush, Bob Dylan, Tom Petty, Eddie Van Halen, and Bono.

First year of production: 1976
Approximate annual production: 6–10
Percent custom instruments: 100
Types of guitars built: Steel-string flattops, 12-strings, nylon-strings, specialty guitars
Primary output: Steel-string flattops
Custom options: Body styles, woods
Guitar pictured: p. 14

Don Musser Guitars
3077 Bird Point Dr. #16
Cotopaxi, CO 81223
Phone: (719) 942-4330

NAPOLITANO GUITARS

Arthur Napolitano began building electric guitars in 1967 and started repairing guitars in 1978. He sold his first archtops in 1973. His guitars represent many influences, including the flattop-building years of Jimmy D'Aquisto and John D'Angelico. Napolitano builds five models, the Primavera, the Acoustic, the Marquee, the Jazz Box Acoustic, and the Jazz Box Electric, and they are all available with a wide variety of options.

First year of production: 1993
Approximate annual production: 24
Percent custom instruments: 100
Types of guitars built: Archtops
Guitar pictured: p. 82

Napolitano Guitars
PO Box 294
Allentown, NJ 08501
Phone/fax: (609) 259-9723

NASHVILLE GUITAR CO.

Marty Lanham has been building stringed instruments since the late 1960s. Lanham moved to Nashville in 1972 to pursue his dream of a music career and was hired by the repair department of GTR (now Gruhn Guitars) the day after he got to town. During his eight years restoring guitars at Gruhn's he was able to handle vast numbers of vintage American-made guitars. He also plays guitar and banjo and spent four years playing banjo as a sideman on the Grand Ole Opry in Nashville. His experience as a player gives him great insight into the intricacies of building musical instruments. In 1980 he started the Nashville Guitar Co.

First year of production: 1970
Approximate annual production: 18
Percent custom instruments: 100
Types of guitars built: Steel-string flattops, specialty guitars
Primary output: Steel-string flattops
Guitar pictured: p. 34

Nashville Guitar Co.
PO Box 160412
Nashville, TN 37216
Phone: (615) 262-4891
www.nashguitar.com

NATIONAL RESO-PHONIC GUITARS

National Reso-Phonic Guitars began in a southern California garage in the spring of 1988. Owners McGregor Gaines and Don Young combined their multifaceted talents to produce the first 12 wood-body resonator guitars, which they brought to an international trade show in January 1989. There they took 50 orders, and the company was launched. Young was first attracted to resonator guitars as a youth when he visited a pawnshop and saw a National guitar. Gaines was trained as an artist, sculptor, and woodworker and is primarily responsible for the aesthetic cohesiveness of the National Reso-Phonic product line. He designs the majority of the custom instruments. Young and Gaines spent many years at Original Musical Instruments (makers of Dobro resophonics), Young as plant supervisor and Gaines as shop foreman, before branching out on their own. They are hands-on owners of their company who draw on a wide range of abilities and creativity in the tooling, fixturing, design, production, and quality control of these unique instruments.

First year of production: 1989
Approximate annual production: 850
Types of guitars built: 12-strings, resonator guitars, specialty guitars
Primary output: Resonators
Custom options: Engraving, fretboard inlays, headstock and heelcap overlays
Guitar pictured: p. 91

National Reso-Phonic Guitars
871-C Via Esteban, Suite C
San Luis Obispo, CA 93401
Phone: (805) 546-8442
Fax: (805) 546-8430
www.nationalguitars.com

NICKERSON GUITARS

Brad Nickerson was born and raised on Cape Cod and showed an early interest in music and the visual arts. He attended the Berklee College of Music and subsequently made his living in the graphic arts field for many years while continuing his interest in music. He built his first guitar in 1982. He received valuable advice and encouragement from New York luthier Carlo Greco as well as Cape Cod violin and bow maker Donald MacKenzie. He found inspiration in James D'Aquisto's innovative ideas and sense of style. Much valuable experience was also gained doing repair work at Bay State Vintage Guitars in Boston and the Fretted Instrument Workshop in Amherst, Massachusetts. Nickerson builds archtop, flattop, and electric guitars on a custom-order basis.

First year of production: 1983
Approximate annual production: 15
Percent custom instruments: 80
Types of guitars built: Steel-string flattops, specialty guitars
Custom options: Scale length, neck width and shape, colors, woods, seven-string, body size and shape
Guitar pictured: p. 87

Nickerson Guitars
8 Easthampton Rd.
Northampton, MA 01060
Phone: (413) 586-8521
www.crocker.com/~archtop

NORTHWORTHY

Northworthy is a small company making some of the highest-quality acoustic guitars available today. The company specializes in steel-string Western-style instruments handmade to order and also produces a range of electric guitars, basses, and folk instruments. Founded in 1987 by Alan Marshall, Northworthy has gained a reputation for building high-quality instruments at sensible prices. The goal is to use some of the finest materials available to produce both highly original and more traditional designs, always striving for sound performance.

First year of production: 1987
Approximate annual production: 35–40
Percent custom instruments: 50
Types of guitars built: Steel-string flattops, 12-strings, nylon-strings, specialty guitars
Primary output: Steel-string flattops
Guitar pictured: p. 20

Northworthy
Main Rd.
Hulland Ward
Ashbourne, Derbyshire DE6 3EA
England
Phone: (44) 1335-370806
Fax: (44) 1335-370932
www.northworthy.com

NOVAX GUITARS

Ralph Novak began doing repairs for local music stores at the age of 16 and began working full-time in a professional capacity in 1976. He worked with Charles LoBue at Alex Music in Manhattan and helped create a new line of Alex Axe pickups and other innovations. He moved to California in 1978 as a partner with LoBue in San Francisco's Guitar Lab and did repairs for Subway Guitars in Berkeley. Novak founded Novax Guitars in 1989 after patenting his fanned fret concept. He received an Industrial Design I.D.E.A. award for the design in 1992. He builds acoustic steel-string flattops; carved archtop acoustic-electrics; and solid-body guitars, baritones, basses, and mandolins featuring the advanced performance of the fanned-fret system. Novax guitars are played by professional musicians of all styles and can be heard on a wide variety of recordings and sound tracks.

First year of production: 1983
Approximate annual production: 10–20
Percent custom instruments: 100
Types of guitars built: Steel-string flattops, archtops, specialty guitars
Primary output: Acoustic-electrics
Custom options: All woods and dimensions
Guitar pictured: p. 100

Novax Guitars
940 A Estabrook
San Leandro, CA 94577
Phone: (510) 483-3599
www.novaxguitars.com

NYBERG INSTRUMENTS

Lawrence Nyberg studied with Michael Dunn for two years and then worked at Larrivée for two years. He builds solid-topped flattop guitars using quality exotic and domestic woods. He spends between four and six weeks building and French-polishing each commission. His style is a combination of the Spanish and North American schools, and he pays special attention to tone; a clean, tasteful aesthetic; quality workmanship; and durability. He uses a scarf-joint headstock, a laminated heel, and spruce liner blocks connecting his soundboards to his sides. He still practices the time-proven technique of using rope and wedges to glue the soundboard and back plates as well as the head-to-neck area. All soundboards and backs are tap-tuned and hand-planed to precise thicknesses. He has extensive experience in shell inlay work and engraving and also uses tagua nut and various exotic wood veneers. Nyberg's tailpieces are an original design and cut from plate brass with a polished copper, brass, gold, or nickel finish. He installs and tweaks all manner of pickup combinations and also offers custom cases.

First year of production: 1993
Approximate annual production: 10–12
Percent custom instruments: 100
Types of guitars built: Steel-string flattops, 12-strings, resonator guitars, specialty guitars
Primary output: Steel-strings and Maccaferri styles
Custom options: Inlays, hardware, pickups, color, and tonal schemes

Nyberg Instruments
6320 Bond Rd.
Hornby Island, BC, Canada
Phone: (250) 335-1727
www.island.net/~nyberg

OLSON GUITARS

Jim Olson is a self-taught guitar maker with a background in furniture making and woodworking. He started building and repairing guitars in the mid-'70s and began Olson Guitars in 1977 as a full-time business. His passion includes designing and building tools, jigs, and fixtures to facilitate his guitar making.

First year of production: 1977
Approximate annual production: 70
Percent custom instruments: 100
Types of guitars built: Steel-string flattops, 12-strings
Custom options: Cutaways, inlays, woods, heel carving
Guitar pictured: p. 41

Olson Guitars
11840 Sunset Ave. N.E.
Circle Pines, MN 55014
Phone: (763) 780-5301
Fax: (763) 780-8513
www.olsonguitars.com

OUTBOUND INSTRUMENTS

First year of production: 1990
Approximate annual production: 200
Percent custom instruments: 10
Types of guitars built: Specialty guitars
Primary output: Travel guitars

Outbound Instruments
5777 Central Ave., Suite 110
Boulder, CO 80301
Phone: (303) 449-1887
Fax: (303) 938-8201

OVATION GUITARS

Ovation builds custom instruments that range from a simple custom color on an otherwise stock instrument to triple-neck six-string/12-string/mandolin instruments built for rock star Richie Sambora. The custom work—everything from computer-generated laser-cut inlays to handmade necks—is done by various craftspeople with special skills. In that sense, the Ovation Custom Shop is more a collection of human resources than a physical work space. Much of the custom designs begin with requests from endorsees (such as Sambora, Preston Reed, and Adrian Legg) but make their way into instruments for other customers as well and often become standard offerings in the Ovation catalog. The Ovation mandolin, for example, began as one-third of the Sambora triple-neck.

First year of production: 1966
Approximate annual production: 60,000
Percent custom instruments: 1
Types of guitars built: Steel-string flattops, 12-strings, nylon-strings, archtops, specialty guitars
Custom options: Double-necks, graphite, etc.
Guitar pictured: p. 102

Ovation Guitars
20 Old Windsor Rd.
Bloomfield, CT 06002-1313
(860) 509-8888
www.kamanmusic.com

SHELLEY D. PARK

Shelley D. Park of Vancouver, British Columbia, began building instruments in 1991, initially studying with Michael Dunn. She had the opportunity to hone her skills in a production environment while working for Larrivée Guitars and gained further valuable experience working in a two-person shop with north Vancouver's David Webber. She has since concentrated on building her own instruments, which embody the classic sound and design of Selmer/Maccaferri guitars built in France during the 1930s and '40s while still reflecting her personal aesthetic and contemporary approach to lutherie. Her models include the Elan, the Encore, and the Advance.

First year of production: 1994

Approximate annual production: 15–20
Percent custom instruments: 100
Types of guitars built: Nylon-strings, specialty guitars
Primary output: Selmer/Maccaferri styles
Guitars pictured: pp. 99, 100

Shelley D. Park
2693 Eton St.
Vancouver, BC V5K 1J9
Canada
Phone: (604) 254-8210
Fax: (604) 299-1746
www.parkguitars.com

PEGASUS GUITARS AND UKULELES

Pegasus Guitars and Ukuleles are made in Kurtistown, Hawaii, by luthier Bob Gleason. Gleason has been building instruments for 28 years and constructs classical and steel-string guitars, as well as all types of ukuleles. He works alone, and production is limited.

First year of production: 1977
Approximate annual production: 12
Percent custom instruments: 100
Types of guitars built: Steel-string flattops, 12-strings, nylon-strings
Custom options: Inlays, woods, designs, electronics

Pegasus Guitars and Ukuleles
PO Box 160
Kurtistown, HI 96760
Phone/fax: (808) 966-6323
www.pegasusguitars.com

PETILLO MASTERPIECE GUITARS

Phillip J. Petillo, an old-fashioned craftsman, mechanical engineer, inventor, draftsman, and musician, started repairing instruments at the age of 14 and began designing and constructing stringed instruments in 1965. He learned from James DiSerio, godson of John D'Angelico, in his Manhattan workshop. Petillo also does restoration work for museums and collectors of antiques and restores vintage harps and bowed stringed instruments. Since 1994, David Petillo has been working on stringed instruments with his father. He specializes in marquetry, mother of pearl, abalone, ivory, and fine inlays of custom design. All Petillo guitars are handmade to suit the customer, and each one is unique. The woods used are between 20 and 100 years old and have been naturally air-dried to insure proper moisture content. The Petillos use Brazilian rosewood, Amazon mahogany, bird's-eye maple, curly maple, German silver spruce, and Nigerian ebony.

First year of production: 1965
Approximate annual production: 10–14
Percent custom instruments: 100
Types of guitars built: Steel-string flattops, 12-strings, nylon-strings, arch-

tops, resonator guitars, Hawaiian guitars, specialty guitars
Guitar pictured: p. 77

Petillo Masterpiece Guitars
1206 Herbert Ave.
Ocean, NJ 07712
Phone: (732) 531-6338
Fax: (732) 531-3045
www.petilloguitars.com

PETROS GUITARS

Bruce Petros discovered his interest in building instruments at the age of 19. He hitchhiked to luthiers' conventions and argued with every guitar builder who would listen. He also read every book available on the subject while constantly building and experimenting. From 1977 to 1992 he built pipe organs with a builder in Appleton, Wisconsin. While honing his instrument-making skills on world-class pipe organs, he was also building his home and dream guitar shop. In 1992 he left the organ shop to resume full-time guitar building. His son Matthew now works full-time for Petros Guitars as well.

First year of production: 1972
Approximate annual production: 24
Percent custom instruments: 25
Types of guitars built: Steel-string flattops, 12-strings, nylon-strings
Primary output: Steel-string flattops
Custom options: Nut width, cutaways, woods, inlays, etc.
Guitar pictured: p. 51

Petros Guitars
345 County Rd. CE
Kaukauna, WI 54130
Phone: (920) 766-1295
Fax: (920) 766-5941
www.petrosguitars.com

PIMENTEL AND SONS

Lorenzo Pimentel began learning the craft of guitar building at the age of 14 in Mexico and emigrated to El Paso, Texas, in 1951, where he founded Pimentel Guitars. He learned his trade through trial and error and taught himself to build guitars of all styles. Eventually he and his family moved to Albuquerque, New Mexico, and Pimentel and Sons was born. From an early age, Pimentel's sons Rick, Robert, Victor, and Lawrence learned to build custom classical guitars. Rick now designs and builds the Southwestern custom series, steel-string flattops, and jazz guitars; Robert builds the Southwestern cutaway electric, classical guitars, flattop steel-strings, and requintos; and Victor and Lawrence build classical and specialty guitars. The woods are aged for ten to 15 years, ensuring beautiful tone and longevity. The guitars are all built by hand, the fingerboard scales are mathematically designed, and the one-of-a-kind inlays are made to each player's specifications. Collectors and concert artists around the world play Pimentel and Sons guitars.

First year of production: 1951
Approximate annual production: 350
Percent custom instruments: 100
Types of guitars built: Steel-string flattops, 12-strings, nylon-strings, archtops, specialty guitars
Primary output: Classicals and flamencos
Guitar pictured: p. 28

Pimentel and Sons
3316 Lafayette Dr. N.E.
Albuquerque, NM 87107
Phone/fax: (505) 884-1669
www.rt66.com/~pimentel

JOHN PRICE

John Price guitars are made with the finest materials, such as Brazilian and other Latin American rosewoods, Western red cedar, German spruce, ebony, and Australian timbers, all seasoned for many years. Lighter soundboards reinforced with carbon fiber and cello-like curved braceless backs combine to give these classical guitars exceptional volume, projection, sustain, clarity, and precision.

First year of production: 1984
Approximate annual production: 24
Percent custom instruments: 100
Types of guitars built: Nylon-strings
Primary output: Classicals and flamencos
Custom options: Arched back, cutaways

John Price
c/o Luthier Music Corp.
341 West 44th St.
New York, NY 10036
Phone: (212) 397-6038/39
Fax: (212) 397-6048
www.luthiermusic.com

QUEEN SHOALS STRINGED INSTRUMENTS

Larry Cadle of Queen Shoals Stringed Instruments began building instruments in 1963 in Clendenin, West Virginia, where he continues to live and work to this day. In his more than three decades of building guitars, he has learned and unlearned volumes about the construction and design of acoustic instruments. His goal is to build dependable instruments with beautiful voices and individual character. He views guitar building as a craft, not an art, and describes himself as a carpenter. His guitars feature nontraditional "ray bracing," and his construction process utilizes computer technology to evaluate bracing schemes, top thicknesses, and top materials.

First year of production: 1972
Approximate annual production: 25–40
Percent custom instruments: 10
Types of guitars built: Steel-string flattops, 12-strings, nylon-strings

Primary output: Steel-string flattops
Guitar pictured: p. 50

Queen Shoals Stringed Instruments
PO Box 658
Clendenin, WV 25045
Phone: (304) 548-6581

QUEGUINER

Although he played steel-string guitar and was a fan of folk music (everything from Bob Dylan to Doc Watson), the first instruments that Alain Queguiner built were classical guitars. The only reference manual available at the time was Irving Sloane's well-known *Classic Guitar Making*. He visited several luthiers in Paris, including Daniel Lesueur, who helped him a great deal. After he built about a dozen classical guitars, Queguiner traveled to San Diego to be trained by Bozo Podunavac. When he returned to France, he gradually developed his own models based on Podunavac's basic construction principles. He currently builds between 12 and 15 guitars per year as well as doing repair and restoration work.

First year of production: 1982
Approximate annual production: 12–15
Percent custom instruments: 100
Types of guitars built: Steel-string flattops, 12-strings
Primary output: Steel-string flattops
Guitar pictured: p. 23

Queguiner
4 Bis Rue Victor Chevrevil
Paris 75012
France
Phone: (33) 01-4341-9513
Fax: (33) 01-4004-9244
www.queguiner.fr.st

JIM REDGATE GUITARS

Australian guitar maker Jim Redgate began his career in music as a classical guitarist. His studies brought him into contact with many fine guitars by makers such as Romanillos, Rubio, Hauser, Fléta, Ramírez, and Smallman, and he found himself doing his own repairs as necessary. He taught himself the fundamentals of guitar construction and attention to detail necessary to build a world-class guitar. Eventually, after building copies of some of these instruments, he began experimenting with new techniques and materials, such as lattice top bracing reinforced with carbon fiber, soundboards with flexible edges to allow the low frequencies to match the increased power of the treble the lattice bracing provides, and soundboards that are typically thicker than other lattice-braced guitars (such as those built by Greg Smallman) but thinner than those of conventional instruments. His insight as a player enables him to competently evaluate his instruments, which is extremely

important in producing fine guitars. Redgate believes that being totally self-taught and living in the relative isolation of Australia has helped him develop new and revolutionary ideas in classical guitar construction.

First year of production: 1992
Approximate annual production: 15
Percent custom instruments: 50
Types of guitars built: Nylon-strings
Primary output: Lattice-braced classicals
Guitars pictured: pp. 52, 53

Jim Redgate Guitars
46 Penno Parade North, Belair
Adelaide South 5052
Australia
Phone/fax: (61) 8-370-3198
www.ozemail.com.au/~redgate/

REUTER GUITARS

John Reuter received a degree in manufacturing engineering technology from Arizona State University in 1982 and worked as a machinist and programmer of CNC machines before enrolling at the Roberto-Venn School of Luthiery. After graduating from Roberto-Venn in 1984 and participating in the graduate workshop program, he was hired on as an instructor. These experiences, along with his impeccable craftsmanship have resulted in improved construction techniques, curriculum revisions, and his promotion to director of training for the Roberto-Venn school in 1995. Reuter guitars have been featured in *Frets* and *Guitarmaker* magazines and have found their way into the hands of fine musicians like Jorma Kaukonen and Joe Myers.

First year of production: 1984
Approximate annual production: 12
Percent custom instruments: 100
Types of guitars built: Steel-string flattops, 12-strings, resonator guitars, Hawaiian guitars, specialty guitars
Primary output: Flattops and resonators
Guitar pictured: p. 92

Reuter Guitars
4011 S. 16th St.
Phoenix, AZ 85040
Phone: (602) 243-1179
Fax: (602) 304-1175
www.roberto-venn.com/jreuter

RANDY REYNOLDS GUITARS

Randy Reynolds is a classical guitar maker in Colorado Springs. He offers several different designs, ranging from traditional Torres/Hauser instruments to contemporary models featuring his own design ideas. His objective is to build a powerful instrument with lots of volume, a rich tonal palette, and a wide dynamic range. He specializes in tailoring sound and playability for each customer and has developed techniques to help players identify

their requirements. He has exhibited guitars at the Healdsburg Guitar Festival in California and is a member of the Colorado Springs Guitar Society, the Black Rose Acoustic Society, the Guitar Foundation of America, the Guild of American Luthiers, and the Association of Stringed Instrument Artisans.

First year of production: 1996
Approximate annual production: 30
Percent custom instruments: 80
Types of guitars built: Steel-string flattops, nylon-strings
Primary output: Classicals and flamencos
Custom options: Woods
Guitar pictured: p. 56

Randy Reynolds Guitars
7168 Milner Dr.
Colorado Springs, CO 80920
Phone: (719) 599-8761
www.reynoldsguitars.com

RIBBECKE GUITARS

Tom Ribbecke's interest in lutherie stems from an early passion for music. He began repairing and building guitars in 1972. His early designs included acoustic steel-strings, solid-body neck-through designs, and his patented Sound Bubble guitars as well as carved archtops and semi-hollow instruments. Ribbecke closed shop in 1983, due to allergic asthma caused by exposure to lacquers and toxic materials, and went to work for Luthiers Mercantile in 1988 as a product consultant. He currently teaches archtop and steel-string guitar building courses, serves as a board member of ASIA, and builds seven different models of instruments in his shop in Healdsburg, California. Players of Ribbecke guitars include Pete Snell, Seal, Jim Adams, Rory Thompson, and Eddie Pasternack.

First year of production: 1972
Approximate annual production: 20
Percent custom instruments: 100
Types of guitars built: Steel-string flattops, archtops, specialty guitars
Primary output: Archtops
Guitar pictured: p. 79

Ribbecke Guitars
PO Box 2215
Healdsburg, CA 95448
Phone: (707) 433-3778
Fax: (707) 433-3778*51
www.ribbecke.com

ROBERTSON GUITARS

Jeff Robertson built his first guitar at the age of seven out of a badminton racquet and two strings. Years later, after earning his B.A. in psychology at Adelphi University, he began building guitars professionally. He built his first guitar with basic woodworking skills, a few hand tools, and a bench that took over his wife's kitchen. He now works full-time as a luthier, building

30 guitars per year in his small shop in upstate New York. He believes that the quality of materials is a vital component of each instrument, and his wife hand-cuts his logos and abalone rosettes. He usually uses select East Indian rosewood and claro walnut for back and sides, Sitka spruce for tops, and Honduran mahogany for necks. He favors two-way adjustable truss rods, bound ebony fingerboards, mother-of-pearl position markers, dovetail neck joints, and nitrocellulose lacquer finishes. His construction techniques combine traditional and innovative methods as well as an uncompromising attention to detail.

First year of production: 1995
Approximate annual production: 30–40
Percent custom instruments: 90
Types of guitars built: Steel-string flat-tops, specialty guitars
Primary output: Steel-string flattops
Custom options: Cutaways, left-handed models, extra bass string, woods, decorative details

Robertson Guitars
505 Bida Rd.
South New Berlin, NY 13843
Phone: (607) 847-9982
www.robertson-guitars.com

GUITARS MANUEL RODRIGUEZ AND SONS

The history of Rodriguez guitars is as rich as the wood used to make the instruments. Grandson of Manuel Rodriguez Marequi, a flamenco guitar player of the last century, and son of Manuel Rodriguez Perez, himself a maker of classic guitars, Manuel Rodriguez learned the art of constructing a guitar first-hand. His apprenticeship began at the age of 13 in Madrid, where he first began to learn what makes a beautiful and resonant guitar. After apprenticing and then operating his own shop in Spain, Rodriguez emigrated to Los Angeles in 1959 and opened a business there. He built guitars for professionals, Hollywood actors, teachers, and students before moving back to Madrid in 1973. He uses only the finest woods and hand-constructs the sides of each guitar to precise tolerances. His distinctive guitars are played by the world's finest artists. Today, as in the past, Rodriguez and his sons put a part of themselves into every guitar they construct. Each is as unique as the musician who plays it.

First year of production: 1905
Approximate annual production: 6
Percent custom instruments: 100
Types of guitars built: Steel-string flat-tops, nylon-strings
Primary output: Classicals and flamencos

Custom options: Inlays, woods, electronics
Guitar pictured: p. 66

Guitars Manuel Rodriguez and Sons
Paseo de Galatea S/N
Esquivias 45221, Toledo
Spain
Phone: (34) 925-520954
Fax: (34) 925-520982

GERMAN VASQUEZ RUBIO

German Vazquez Rubio was born in 1952 in Paracho, Minoacan, Mexico. He began building classical and flamenco guitars in 1968, working alongside his uncle Manuel Rubio. He continued his studies with eminent Madrid maker Felix Manzanero, English builder José Luis Romanillos, and U.S. builder Thomas Humphrey. His instruments have been exhibited at many festivals and gatherings, including the Guitar Foundation of America, the Boston Guitar Mini-Fest, the Ithaca Guitar Festival, and the Stetson Guitar Festival. His guitars are sought for their musical refinement, dynamic range, balance, and elegant craftsmanship. They are played by such renowned professionals as Liona Boyd, Freddy Bryant, Ricardo Cobo, Kirk Hanser, and Jason Vieaux.

First year of production: 1993
Approximate annual production: 100
Percent custom instruments: 15
Types of guitars built: Classicals and flamencos
Custom options: Scale length, fingerboard width, inlays, woods, bracing patterns, handmade machine heads
Guitar pictured: p. 54

German Vazquez Rubio
C/o Guitars International
22625 Westchester Rd.
Cleveland, OH 44122
Phone: (216) 752-7502
Fax: (216) 752-7593
www.guitars-int.com

ROBERT RUCK

Robert Ruck attended the Milwaukee Conservatory of Music, learned the fundamentals of fine woodworking from John Shaw, and began building guitars full-time at the age of 20. Over the past 30 years, he has built more than 740 guitars as well as lutes, dulcimers, viola da gambas, and vihuelas. He continues to play classical and flamenco guitar when he's not busy in the shop. Ruck's instruments begin with a specific sound he aspires to create. From there he chooses the woods and decides on the key design elements that will shape the sound he is after.

First year of production: 1966
Approximate annual production: 25–30
Types of guitars built: Nylon-strings
Primary output: Classicals and flamencos
Guitar pictured: p. 56

Robert Ruck
5805 Minder Rd. N.E. #3
Poulsbo, WA 98370
Phone: (360) 297-4024
Fax: (360) 297-4405

RUNNING DOG GUITARS

Rick Davis came to guitar making after 20 years of professional woodworking (building furniture and small boats) and five years as the assistant director of the University of Vermont's performing arts series. He had met luthier John Greven some years earlier and realized then that you don't need a factory to build fine guitars. Leaving the university gave him the time to pursue his dream of making his own instruments. He now serves as director of the Association of Stringed Instrument Artisans and editor of *Guitarmaker* magazine. Running Dog guitars are known for two things: small bodies and imaginative use of alternative woods. These reflect Davis' personal concern for careful conservation of our forests and valuable timbers and his preference for the superior tone and playability of well-made smaller instruments. He custom-builds all Running Dog guitars, so there are no stock models. Each instrument is built for the particular needs of the player, and only 12 commissions are accepted per year. Wood bindings and rosettes, necks shaped to the desires of the player, a bound fingerboard, and choice of purfling and inlay patterns are standard features on Running Dog guitars.

First year of production: 1994
Approximate annual production: 12
Percent custom instruments: 100
Types of guitars built: Steel-string flattops
Primary output: Small-bodies
Guitar pictured: p. 42

Running Dog Guitars
1394 Stage Rd.
Richmond, VT 05477
Phone: (802) 434-4399
Fax: (802) 434-5657
www.vtguitars.com

KEVIN RYAN GUITARS

Kevin Ryan has been building guitars since 1987 and is established as one of the world's premier luthiers. His background as a fingerstyle guitarist and aerospace researcher lends his guitar making a unique creativity and precision. He has built instruments for some of this century's finest fingerstyle players, including Peter Finger, Laurence Juber, Isato Nakagawa, Franco Morone, Woody Mann, and five Winfield National Champions: Pat Donohue, Muriel Anderson, Charles David Alexander, Eric Lugosch, and Tim Sparks. He also built instruments for singer-songwriters Jackson Browne, Janis Ian, Bob Bennett, and Steve Bell. Ryan guitars are known for their responsiveness, clarity, beauty, playability, and tone. They feature custom scale lengths, sleek necks made possible by innovative engineering, and Ryan's signature arch-swept back. Ryan's models include the Mission Grand Concert, the Cathedral Grand Fingerstyle, and the Sanctuario Grand Parlor.

First year of production: 1989
Approximate annual production: 40–60
Percent custom instruments: 100
Types of guitars built: Steel-string flattops
Custom options: Cutaways, woods, inlays, neck profile, nut width, scale length, and body style
Guitars pictured: pp. 11, 39

Kevin Ryan Guitars
14211 Wiltshire St.
Westminster, CA 92683
Phone: (714) 379-0944
www.ryanguitars.com

SAHLIN GUITARS

Eric Sahlin was born in 1956 in Spokane, Washington. He is a self-taught craftsman, who developed an interest in woodworking at an early age. In 1977 he began building custom furniture as well as guitars, and he switched to building only musical instruments after a few years. He has built steel-strings and lutes but has concentrated his efforts on the construction of classical guitars since the mid-'80s.

First year of production: 1975
Approximate annual production: 16
Percent custom instruments: 100
Types of guitars built: Nylon-strings
Primary output: Classicals and flamencos
Custom options: Multiple bass strings, woods, inlays, rosettes

Sahlin Guitars
4324 E. 37th Ave.
Spokane, WA 99223
Phone/fax: (509) 448-4024

TAKU SAKASHTA

Taku Sakashta became interested in guitars at the age of ten in his hometown of Kobe, Japan. He attended engineering and design school in Japan and then spent five years developing a curriculum for teaching guitar making at the school. Over the next eight years, he worked for major guitar companies, designing, developing, and producing custom professional guitars for musicians. He came to the United States in 1991 and started his own guitar-making business. In 1996 he moved to Sonoma, California, where he presently designs and builds all types of guitars, using only the highest-quality materials and finishes. He works one-on-one with his customers to determine specifications for all his custom guitar designs. Whether working with modern or classic guitar designs, his goal is always to achieve perfection in sound, construction, decoration, and finish. His clients include Tony Darren, Robben Ford, Tony Marcus, Boz Scaggs, and Martin Simpson.

First year of production: 1994
Approximate annual production: 15–20
Percent custom instruments: 75
Types of guitars built: Steel-string flattops, 12-strings, nylon-strings, archtops, specialty guitars
Primary output: Archtops
Guitar pictured: p. 87

Taku Sakashta
PO Box 1851
Sonoma, CA 95476
Phone: (707) 938-8604
Fax: (707) 938-5246
www.sakashtaguitars.com

SANTA CRUZ GUITAR CO.

Richard Hoover began building guitars and carved-top mandolins in 1972. By 1976 his focus had shifted to the modern steel-string guitar. Mastering all aspects of guitar making is a lifelong pursuit, and Hoover is patiently refining his craftsmanship and knowledge as his company grows. His goal is to translate his own skills and sensitivities as an individual builder to an exceptional team of craftspeople, each of whom becomes an expert in his or her specialty. Hoover allows his craftspeople to interpret his vision for themselves, and this group dynamic has propelled the Santa Cruz Guitar Co. to the forefront of modern guitar making. Each Santa Cruz guitar receives an extraordinary amount of individual attention. Over half of Santa Cruz guitars are custom orders that reflect the personality and playing needs of the buyer. Every guitar top is graduated and tuned by hand to attain maximum resonance and sustain, ensuring consistency of sound. The balance, tone, volume, and response of a Santa Cruz guitar are established before the guitar is strung. The overarching goal is to create a sophisticated instrument that will inspire and challenge its owner throughout his or her lifetime.

First year of production: 1977
Approximate annual production: 750
Percent custom instruments: 50
Types of guitars built: Steel-string flattops, 12-strings, archtops, specialty guitars
Custom options: Woods, inlays, bracing pattern, 12-strings, cutaways, etc.
Guitar pictured: p. 25

Santa Cruz Guitar Co.
328 Ingalls Ave.
Santa Cruz, CA 95060
Phone: (831) 425-0999
Fax: (831) 425-3604
www.santacruzguitar.com

SCHEERHORN GUITARS

Tim Scheerhorn has been building instruments since 1989. He was inspired to build resonator guitars when he was unable to find good ones for his own playing needs. He transformed the resonator design with unique internal baffling and the elimination of the traditional soundwell. His guitars are played by Jerry Douglas, Rob Ickes, Sally Van Meter, Phil Leadbetter, Mike Auldridge, Jimmy Stewart, Randy Kohrs, and others who earn their living playing music. Scheerhorn's is a one-man shop, where he produces approximately 45 instruments per year.

First year of production: 1989
Approximate annual production: 45–50
Percent custom instruments: 100
Types of guitars built: Resonator guitars, Hawaiian guitars
Primary output: Resonators
Guitars pictured: pp. 93, 94

Scheerhorn Guitars
1454 52nd St.
Kentwood, MI 49508
Phone: (616) 281-3927

SCHOENBERG GUITARS

Schoenberg guitars are the culmination of fingerstyle guitarist Eric Schoenberg's three-decade search for the perfect fingerpicking guitar. His company was originally formed in 1986 to manufacture vintage-style OM guitars in conjunction with C.F. Martin and Co. Schoenberg believes that the OM's design represents the true golden era of modern guitar making. These guitars are light enough to be played without picks and respond fully to the lightest touch, but they also display full power and clarity when played strongly. Schoenberg guitars are built in a small shop in Littleton, Massachusetts, under the leadership of Julius Borges, and Schoenberg markets the instruments from Tiburon, California.

First year of production: 1987
Approximate annual production: 40
Percent custom instruments: 25
Types of guitars built: Steel-string flattops
Custom options: Body style, woods, neck dimensions, inlays
Guitar pictured: p. 35

Schoenberg Guitars
106 Main St.
Tiburon, CA 94920
Phone: (415) 789-0846
Fax: (415) 789-0116
www.schoenbergguitars.com

SCHRAMM GUITARS

David Schramm began building guitars in 1990 while completing his B.A. in classical guitar performance. He was always fascinated by woodworking and had earned prizes during high school for his homemade furniture.

Schramm plays many musical instruments, including violin, piano, trumpet, trombone, and guitar. He excelled right from the start as a luthier, and the demand for his instruments is always growing. He cites guitar maker John Gilbert, with whom he has studied and consulted, as one of his main influences, especially in terms of bridge design. In 1993 Schramm was chosen to be the first authorized American luthier to build the GRANguitar (Guitar Russian Acoustically New), a hybrid steel and nylon 12-string created by Anatoliy Olshanskiy and Vladimir Ustinov. Schramm is the foremost American authority on the history, construction, and performance techniques related to this instrument.

First year of production: 1990
Approximate annual production: 20
Percent custom instruments: 25
Types of guitars built: Nylon-strings, specialty guitars
Primary output: Classicals and flamencos
Custom options: Split 20th fret, historic reproductions, cutaways, handcrafted flamenco tuning pegs, Gilbert saddle pin bridges.
Guitar pictured: p. 64

Schramm Guitars
926 W. Princeton Ave.
Fresno, CA 93705
Phone: (559) 244-0815
www.schrammguitars.com

SCHRODER GUITARS

Timothy Schröder opened his shop in the Chicago area in the summer of 1993 to custom-build, repair, and restore professional-quality instruments. He began his training at the Gibson factory warranty facility in Spring Hill, Tennessee, and then went to work for master repairman Gary Brawer, whose San Francisco, California, shop serviced such clientele as the Grateful Dead, Joe Satriani, and Albert Collins, as well as many Windham Hill artists. He then studied archtop construction with master luthier Robert Benedetto. Schröder musical instruments are individually crafted from master-grade spruce, maple, and ebony. Long seasoning treatments and rigorous checks guarantee both quality and lasting durability. The entire design results from the requirements of sound.

First year of production: 1993
Approximate annual production: 12–20
Percent custom instruments: 50
Types of guitars built: Archtops
Custom options: Inlays
Guitar pictured: p. 76

Schröder Guitars
1856 Techny Ct.
Northbrook, IL 60062
Phone: (847) 509-8930
www.archtopguitars.com

SCHWARTZ GUITARS

Sheldon Schwartz builds guitars using only top-quality materials and techniques that combine the best of old-world craftsmanship with the latest in guitar-building technology. He has learned from guitar builders Grit Laskin, Linda Manzer, and Kent Everett and has been a professional luthier himself since 1993. Schwartz guitars look traditional but feature Schwartz' original designs. He has borrowed from the best hand-builders of classical guitars such techniques as using the lightest possible clamping pressure during assembly, which results in stress-free parts that are free to vibrate. Schwartz guitars feature wood bindings, a solid interior lining, a bound fingerboard, rounded fret ends, and a high-gloss lacquer finish. Each soundboard and back is individually thicknessed and tap-tuned to get the best tone from the wood, and meticulous attention is paid to every detail of the construction process.

First year of production: 1992
Approximate annual production: 8–12
Percent custom instruments: 100
Types of guitars built: Steel-string flattops, 12-strings
Primary output: Steel-string flattops
Custom options: Cutaways, woods, abalone top trim, inlays and engraving, headstock shapes, etc.
Guitar pictured: p. 41

Schwartz Guitars
371 Bradwick Dr., Unit 5
Concord, ON L4K 2P4
Canada
Phone: (905) 738-0024
Fax: (905) 738-8129
www.schwartzguitars.com

SERGE GUITARS

Sergé Michaud was introduced to woodworking by his father, a professional cabinetmaker and wood turner. Michaud obtained a B.A. in engineering and worked as an engineer for ten years before studying the craft of lutherie. After building his first instrument with the help of a book, he attended a guitar-building seminar in 1995 at Timeless Instruments. He now runs a complete guitar-building shop and lutherie school, Sergé Guitars, in Breakeyville, Quebec, and is a member of GAL and ASIA.

First year of production: 1995
Approximate annual production: 30
Percent custom instruments: 15
Types of guitars built: Steel-string flattops, nylon-strings, archtops, resonator guitars
Primary output: Steel-string flattops

Sergé Guitars
50 Boutin Sud Ave.
Breakeyville, PQ G0S 1E3
Canada
Phone: (418) 832-6080
www3.sympatico.ca/smichaud

SEXAUER GUITARS

Bruce Sexauer has been playing guitar since he was 17 and began building instruments in 1967 to satisfy his own need for a better instrument. He started with solid-body guitars and then moved to dulcimers and flattops, always working with his own designs. He went on to build psalteries, mandolins, a tiple, a guitarron, and two full-sized harps in addition to a steady stream of individually built flattops. In the '90s he discovered a passion for building archtop guitars and has developed a design that offers clarity, sensitivity, and volume and is influenced by Selmer/Maccaferri guitars as well as certain Larson Brothers models from the '30s. The result is Sexauer's Coo'stic Dominator, an induced-arch guitar with a clear tone, delicate touch, and plenty of overhead.

First year of production: 1967
Approximate annual production: 12
Percent custom instruments: 100
Types of guitars built: Steel-string flattops, 12-strings, nylon-strings, archtops, specialty guitars
Primary output: Steel-string flattops

Sexauer Guitars
724 H St.
Petaluma, CA 94952
Phone: (707) 782-1044
www.sexauerluthier.com

SHANTI GUITARS

Michael Hornick was a woodworker for many years before he began building guitars in 1984. Since then he has been building steel-string guitars and lecturing at various schools of lutherie. He is basically self-taught, although Richard Hoover of the Santa Cruz Guitar Co. has acted as his mentor for many years.

First year of production: 1985
Approximate annual production: 8
Percent custom instruments: 100
Types of guitars built: Steel-string flattops, 12-strings, nylon-strings
Primary output: Steel-string flattops
Custom options: Every aspect of guitar
Guitar pictured: p. 22

Shanti Guitars
PO Box 341
Avery, CA 95224
Phone: (209) 795-5299

SHIFFLETT GUITARS

Charles Shifflett built his first guitar in 1990 while studying musical instrument construction at Douglas College in New Westminster, B.C. Schooled in the Spanish tradition, Shifflett favors light construction, the Spanish heel, French polish, and exotic hardwood binding instead of plastics. He enjoys guiding his customers through the many choices that ultimately result in an instrument built to suit the player's particular needs. In recent years, his focus has returned to classic and Maccaferri-style guitars. His influences include Antonio de Torres, Louis Panormo, Jose Romanillos, Geza Burghardt, and Michael Dunn.

First year of production: 1990
Approximate annual production: 5–8
Percent custom instruments: 100
Types of guitars built: Steel-string flattops, nylon-strings
Primary output: Classicals and flamencos
Custom options: Woods, etc.
Guitars pictured: pp. 60, 70

Shifflett Guitars
124 7 Ave. West
High River, AB T1V 1A2
Canada
Phone: (403) 652-1526
http://ourworld.compuserve.com/
homepages/cshifflett

MARC SILBER GUITAR CO.

Marc Silber became interested in building guitars in 1960 when he first visited Lundberg Fretted Instruments in Berkeley, California. His first efforts involved modifying existing guitars, rather than building new instruments from scratch. He converted Kays and Harmony Sovereigns into 12-strings, extending the pegheads and adding new veneers. He went to work for Lundberg in the repair department, where he encountered the work of classical guitar maker Eugene Clark. Clark taught Silber a lot about building fine guitars. Silber then moved to New York City, where he and Izzy Young opened Fretted Instruments, a guitar shop in Greenwich Village in November 1963. He left the lutherie business five years later only to return as a dealer several years later, focusing on inexpensive instruments such as Stellas. In 1987 he began selling instruments by appointment in Berkeley, California. His business provides beautiful, handmade acoustic guitars, Hawaiian guitars, and ukuleles at relatively low prices.

First year of production: 1992
Approximate annual production: 30–50
Percent custom instruments: 0
Types of guitars built: Steel-string flattops, nylon-strings, Hawaiian guitars
Guitars pictured: pp. 68, 97

Marc Silber Guitar Co.
930 Dwight Way #9
Berkeley, CA 94710
Phone/fax: (510) 664-1958
www.marcsilbermusic.com

GEORGE SMITH

George Smith began repairing instruments in 1957. He learned how instruments are constructed by taking them apart and putting them back together. As public interest in folk music grew, so did interest in his repair work. There was a shortage of old-style instruments at the time, such as 12-string guitars and five-string banjos, and he began filling the demand with modified and newly built instruments. He also learned to build classical guitars, hammer dulcimers, lutes, and harpsichords. Recently, he has limited his building to classical and flamenco guitars, which are based on a modified Torres/Hauser design. Each instrument is made with carefully selected woods from his own stock. Tops and backs are weighed and measured for stiffness both with and across the grain. Tops are graduated and all measurements are noted for future reference. Each instrument Smith builds has its own file. Careful workmanship and intuition from years of experience help him achieve the sound and visual qualities that satisfy his customers.

First year of production: 1959
Approximate annual production: 6–9
Percent custom instruments: 100
Types of guitars built: Nylon-strings
Primary output: Classicals and flamencos
Custom options: Woods, tuning machines, inlays
Guitar pictured: p. 66

George Smith
1391 S.W. Broadway Dr.
Portland, OR 97201
Phone: (503) 228-3570
www.jps.net/kashka

LAWRENCE K. SMITH

Lawrence Smith built his first instrument, a lute constructed from a kit, in 1977. In 1989 he decided to devote all his time to making fine guitars and mandolins. He has built a wide variety of stringed instruments, including lutes, charangos, and vihuelas, but he now makes only limited-edition concert classical guitars, acoustic guitars, and archtops. Smith is past president of AAMIM, the Australian Association of Musical Instrument Makers. A player himself, he has very high standards for his instruments' tone and playability. He tunes the modes of the soundboard and air cavities in his instruments to optimize their acoustic potential. His love of wood has led him to search out and select some of the finest timbers available from around the world.

First year of production: 1978
Approximate annual production: 10–14
Percent custom instruments: 50
Types of guitars built: Steel-string flattops, nylon-strings, archtops
Custom options: Pearl inlay, purfling, cutaways, sunburst finish

Lawrence K. Smith
8 Mt. Gilead Rd.
Thirrow, NSW 2515
Australia
Phone/fax: (61) 2-4267-2392
www.smithguitars.com

STEFAN SOBELL MUSICAL INSTRUMENTS

Stefan Sobell began building mandolin-family instruments in the early 1970s, introducing the modern cittern in 1973. He moved on to building round-hole archtops in 1982 and flattops in 1983. One of his signature features is his heavily curved soundboard and back, which require minimum internal tension. Martin Simpson has been playing Sobell guitars since 1984.

First year of production: 1982
Approximate annual production: 40
Percent custom instruments: 90
Types of guitars built: Steel-string flattops, 12-strings, archtops
Guitar pictured: p. 76

Stefan Sobell Musical Instruments
The Old School
Whitley Chapel
Hetham, Northumberland NE47 OHB
England
Phone/fax: (44) 1434-673567
www.sobellinstruments.com

SON FATHER GUITARS

David A. Cassotta included his father in the name of his business as thanks for the many lessons in quality craftsmanship he learned from him. Cassotta began building guitars in the early '90s and became a full-time professional luthier in 1994. His first shop was a converted garage, and he now works out of a much larger commercial shop with a retail showroom. He offers two D models, two 00s, nylon-string guitars, and custom-designed acoustic and electric guitars.

First year of production: 1994
Approximate annual production: 12
Percent custom instruments: 10
Types of guitars built: Steel-string flattops, 12-strings, nylon-strings
Primary output: Steel-string flattops
Custom options: Pearl and abalone inlay, wood binding and purfling, rosettes

Son Father Guitars
4930 Pacific St.
Rocklin, CA 95677
Phone: (916) 624-3794
Fax: (916) 624-5688
www.sonfatherguitars.com

GARY SOUTHWELL

A passion for playing guitars combined with a love of wood inspired Gary Southwell to study guitar making at the London College of Furniture. He set up his own workshop in 1983 and devoted his early years as a luthier to making and restoring early 19th-century guitars. He has working drawings and detailed documentation on a large number of extant instruments from various museums and private collections around the world, and he writes, lectures, and acts as a consultant on the topic. This unique perspective informs the designs he uses to build his modern classical guitars, which are played by some of the finest musicians in the world. Southwell is constantly testing new ideas and designs, always striving to improve sound quality, playability, and aesthetics. He enjoys working on unusual one-off instruments and worked closely with musician David Starobin to develop his A series guitars, with Julian Bream to reproduce Hauser guitars, and with Jim Kiln on the unusual 11-string Arch guitar. Such collaboration enables a fascinating exchange of ideas, which is reflected in all the work Southwell produces.

First year of production: 1983
Approximate annual production: 12
Percent custom instruments: 100
Types of guitars built: Nylon-strings, specialty guitars
Primary output: Classicals
Guitar pictured: p. 66

Gary Southwell
12 Chaucer Court Workshops
Chaucer St.
Nottingham NG1 5LP
England
Phone: (44) 115-947-3633
Fax: (44) 115-982-1637
www.garysguitars.cwc.net

STANSELL GUITARS

Les Stansell makes his living on the southern Oregon coast creating guitars, unique cabinetry, and custom homes. He believes that building instruments is the ultimate woodworking experience and that Spanish-style classicals are the ultimate guitars. His goal is to build light and powerful instruments that allow the woods to realize their full potential. He studied under Anthony Huvard at the Northwest School of Instrument Design in Seattle in the late '70s and in Skykomish, Washington, in 1981.

First year of production: 1980
Approximate annual production: 10–12
Percent custom instruments: 100
Types of guitars built: Nylon-strings
Primary output: Classicals
Custom options: Rosettes, headstocks, woods, neck shapes, string length, finish, purfling
Guitar pictured: p. 67

Stansell Guitars
95100 S. Pistol River Rd.
Pistol River, OR 97444
Phone/fax: (541) 247-7636
www.stansellguitars.com

THOMPSON GUITARS

Ted Thompson went to Spain, got inspired, came home, and started building classical guitars. He added steel-strings to his line and then got into electric guitars in the mid-'80s.

First year of production: 1980
Approximate annual production: 100
Percent custom instruments: 20
Types of guitars built: Steel-string flat-tops, 12-strings, nylon-strings
Primary output: Steel-string flattops
Custom options: String length, fingerboard width, neck shape, inlays, woods

Thompson Guitars
9905 Coldstream Creek Rd.
Vernon, BC V1B 1C8
Canada
Phone/fax: (250) 542-9410

THREET GUITARS

In the late '80s, while teaching philosophy at the University of Calgary, Judy Threet learned the principles of inlay from Michael Heiden. By 1990, Heiden had overseen the building of her first guitar, and by 1991 Threet had switched careers and begun her own guitar-making shop. Her individually handcrafted instruments range in size from parlor guitars to dreadnoughts and are played across North America and Japan. She completes approximately 12 instruments per year, working in a warehouse loft in one of Calgary's oldest areas, and offers a wide variety of custom options and custom inlays. She hand-carves the necks of her instruments to suit the player's wishes and carefully voices each top to maximize both sustain and separation. The result is a guitar particularly well-suited to fingerstyle playing.

First year of production: 1994
Approximate annual production: 10
Percent custom instruments: 60
Types of guitars built: Steel-string flattops
Custom options: Woods, decorative touches, neck shapes, nut widths, string spacing
Guitar pictured: p. 26

Threet Guitars
1215 13th St. S.E.
Calgary, AB T2G 3J4
Canada
Phone/fax: (403) 232-8332
www.threetguitars.com

TIMELESS INSTRUMENTS

David Freeman began repairing instruments in 1978 and building them in 1980. His background is in furniture refinishing and restoration, woodcarving, sculpture, and pottery, and he studied with George Morris and Charles Fox at Vermont's School of Guitar Repair and Design before returning to Saskatchewan in 1980 to start Timeless Instruments. He established his own lutherie school in 1986 and began a mail-order luthier supply business in 1987. Freeman has never built the same instrument twice. There are certain body shapes and woods that he favors, but the bracing structure for each instrument is unique and achieves specific sound requirements. He builds mainly steel-string and classical guitars but has also constructed bouzoukis, citterns, mandolins, harps, and dulcimers. Freeman sells his instruments direct and enjoys consulting with customers on the design of their instrument.

First year of production: 1980
Approximate annual production: 30
Percent custom instruments: 100
Types of guitars built: Steel-string flat-tops, 12-strings, nylon-strings, resonator guitars, specialty guitars
Primary output: Steel-string flattops
Guitar pictured: p. 32

Timeless Instruments
341 Bison St.
Tugaske, SK S0H 4B0
Canada
Phone: (306) 759-2042
Fax: (306) 759-2729
www3.sk.sympatico.ca/timeless

TIMM GUITARS

Jerry Timm began designing and building fine custom furniture in 1981 and built his first acoustic guitar in the mid-'90s. He produces about a dozen guitars per year, primarily custom instruments, and focuses on playability and tone quality.

First year of production: 1997
Approximate annual production: 12
Percent custom instruments: 100
Types of guitars built: Steel-string flat-tops, resonator guitars, specialty guitars
Primary output: Resonators and travel guitars
Custom options: Cutaways, abalone and MOP inlays, woods, body specs
Guitasr pictured: cover, p. 90

Timm Guitars
4512 47th St. S.E.
Auburn, WA 98092
Phone: (253) 833-8667
Fax: (253) 833-1820
www.timmguitars.com

TIPPIN GUITAR CO.

Bill Tippin's background is in furniture making and boat building. His first guitar was built from a Martin kit. He went on to read every book on guitar building that he could find and to experiment with his own guitar designs and construction techniques. Word spread, and the Tippin Guitar Co. was launched in 1978. Each Tippin guitar is constructed with individually selected woods, the finest hardware, and Tippin's exacting standards. The learning process never ends: each guitar benefits from the ones that were built before it. Tippin and his crew consistently produce guitars with a balanced sound and a graceful, traditional look.

First year of production: 1978
Approximate annual production: 50
Percent custom instruments: 60
Types of guitars built: Steel-string flat-tops, specialty guitars
Custom options: Pearl inlay, woods, neck shapes, body depth, tuners, etc.
Guitar pictured: p. 38

Tippin Guitar Co.
3 Beacon St.
Marblehead, MA 01945
Phone: (781) 631-5749
Fax: (781) 639-0934
www.tippinguitar.com

DAKE TRAPHAGEN

Dake Traphagen began building folk stringed instruments in 1970 and then served a challenging two-year apprenticeship in violin making and restoration with Ed Huntington. He became interested in building classical, flamenco, and Baroque guitars, as well as lutes, harpsichords, and other early stringed instruments. He worked with Dutch luthier Nico van der Waals in the mid-'70s and moved to Bellingham, Washington, in 1978. Since then he has focused almost exclusively on building classical guitars. Many concert players use his instruments, including Pepe Romeo, Scott Tennant, Michael Lucarelli, and Andrew Schulman.

First year of production: 1972
Approximate annual production: 20
Percent custom instruments: 100
Types of guitars built: Nylon-strings, specialty guitars
Primary output: Classicals
Custom options: String length, neck shapes, woods
Guitar pictured: p. 55

Dake Traphagen
916 Harris Ave.
Bellingham, WA 98225
Phone: (360) 671-1017
www.traphagenguitars.com

JEFF TRAUGOTT GUITARS

While studying music at Evergreen State College in Olympia, Washington, Jeff Traugott became fascinated with the art of lutherie. He moved to Santa Cruz, California, and opened a small music store catering to acoustic string players in 1984. He began working for the Santa Cruz Guitar Co. in 1986 and left in 1991 to open his own shop, which is located in an old industrial complex that now houses a diverse community of artisans and craftspeople. He moved into the empty shell and proceeded to design and build his dream guitar shop. While he was developing his work space, the bulk of Traugott's production consisted of repairing old Martins and other high-end acoustic guitars. Recent projects include experiments with Ralph Novak's fanned-fret system and work on a multineck guitar for professional player Benjamin Verdery. Traugott's guitars have a clean, classic look and feature excellent tone and playability.

First year of production: 1991
Approximate annual production: 20
Percent custom instruments: 100

Types of guitars built: Steel-string flat-tops, 12-strings, nylon-strings, arch-tops, specialty guitars

Primary output: Steel-string flattops

Guitar pictured: p. 10

Jeff Traugott Guitars
2553 B Mission St.
Santa Cruz, CA 95060
Phone: (831) 426-2313
Fax: (831) 426-0187
www.traugottguitars.com

TRUE NORTH GUITARS

Dennis Scannell is an MIT graduate and master woodworker who has played and worked on guitars since the early 1970s. In 1994 he established his lutherie business, focusing on high-quality steel-string guitars for fingerstyle players who favor altered tunings. He has been a member of ASIA since 1994 and the GAL since 1995, the same year he attended the American School of Lutherie. Since then Scannell has attended numerous ASIA symposia and GAL conventions, refined his technique through further study of individual aspects of guitar making, developed his inventory of master-quality tonewoods and materials, and completed his guitar studio in northern Vermont. He introduced his True North guitars at the 1999 Healdsburg Guitar Festival. Standard appointments of True North guitars include ergonomic, side-tapered bodies; hand-voiced, radiused soundboards with scalloped braces and sculpted X-brace joints; fast, graphite-reinforced necks; bound fingerboards with semi-hemispherical frets; extended scales; asymmetrical head-stocks; green heart abalone trim; and elegant, mathematically pure lines. True North guitars offer a well-balanced, articulate voice with an open airy bass, pristine highs, and a smooth expressive midrange. They are meant to be played and loved for a lifetime.

First year of production: 1999

Approximate annual production: 8

Percent custom instruments: 100

Types of guitars built: Steel-string flattops

Guitar pictured: p. 29

True North Guitars
175 Perry Lea Side Rd.
Waterbury, VT 05676
Phone/fax: (802) 244-6488
www.truenorthguitars.com

TURNER GUITARS

Rick Turner started disassembling and crudely restoring instruments while still in high school in the late 1950s. In 1963 he apprenticed as a repairman in a Boston, Massachusetts, shop while developing his guitar playing chops. He went on the road with Canadian folksingers Ian and Sylvia in 1965 and recorded two albums with them on the Vanguard label. He began building acoustic and then electric guitars in 1968 and in 1970 co-founded Alembic, developing a full line of electric basses and guitars that are still in production. In 1978 he founded Turner Guitars and designed the instrument now associated with Lindsey Buckingham of Fleetwood Mac. He spent eight years away from the guitar business before doing some R&D work for Gibson and taking over the repair department at Westwood Music in L.A. Today Turner custom-builds approximately six acoustic guitars per year while running the Renaissance Guitar Co., which has been producing top-of-the-line amplicoustic guitars since 1994. His client list includes such notable players as David Crosby, Ry Cooder, Jackson Browne, Stanley Clarke, Graham Nash, and Ali Farka Toure. Turner also writes for various music magazines and has been a contributing editor to *Acoustic Guitar* since 1991.

First year of production: 1968

Approximate annual production: 6

Percent custom instruments: 100

Types of guitars built: Steel-string flat-tops, 12-strings, nylon-strings, arch-tops, specialty guitars

Guitars pictured: pp. 36, 101

Turner Guitars
815 Almar St.
Santa Cruz, CA 95060
Phone: (831) 460-9144
Fax: (831) 460-9146
www.rickturnerguitars.com

CHARLES VEGA

Charles Vega has been building and repairing acoustic guitars since the early 1970s. His primary focus is on traditional classical and flamenco guitars, which he began building in earnest in 1993. More recently he has concentrated on specialty and one-off variants of the classical guitar. Although primarily self-taught, Vega has learned from every luthier he's ever met and has visited the shops of some of the prominent guitar makers in Spain. He uses very few jigs, fixtures, or power tools in his work, generally building guitars in the Spanish style without the use of forms or molds. He firmly believes in using nontraditional woods.

First year of production: 1993

Approximate annual production: 8–10

Percent custom instruments: 50

Types of guitars built: Nylon-strings, specialty guitars

Primary output: Classicals and flamencos

Custom options: Woods, scale length, tuners, body shapes

Guitar pictured: p. 107

Charles Vega
2101 Carterdale Rd.
Baltimore, MD 21209-4523
Phone: (410) 664-6506
Fax: (410) 516-8429

VERSOUL, LTD.

Versoul is a small company specializing in high-end guitars for professional musicians. The company's founder, Kari Nieminen, has more than 20 years of experience in the field and an M.F.A. in industrial design. In 1998 he was awarded Industrial Designer of the Year in his native Finland, and in 1999 his Zoel model steel-string flattop was featured on a postage stamp showcasing new Finnish design. Versoul instruments have been displayed in national and international design exhibitions, including Spain's Sevilla Expo World Fair. They are featured on hundreds of professional recordings and played on stages throughout Europe and the United States. Players of Versoul guitars include Terry Britten, Crispin Mills, Amancio Prada, Pete Brewis, Will McRory Rogers, Stanley Clarke, Brian Wilson, Rod Stewart, and Barry Hay of Golden Earring.

First year of production: 1994

Approximate annual production: 30–40

Percent custom instruments: 25

Types of guitars built: Steel-string flat-tops, 12-strings, nylon-strings, arch-tops, specialty guitars

Custom options: Inlays

Versoul, Ltd.
Kutomotie 13 C
Helsinki, Finland
FIN-00380
Phone/fax: (358) 9-565-1876
www.kolumbus.fi/versoul

WALKER GUITARS

Kim Walker has been a full-time guitar builder since 1974. In 1979, he moved to Nashville to work for noted dealer George Gruhn, where he ran the repair shop and restored some of the world's most legendary guitars. "Kim is one of the finest craftsmen I have ever met," says Gruhn. "His workmanship and sense of aesthetics are truly extraordinary." In 1987 Walker moved to New England to work for Guild Guitars, working variously on R&D, custom work, production, quality control, and as assistant plant manager. Some of the models he built prototypes for are still in production today. He left Guild in 1994 and expanded his home-based custom business to a full-time venture, drawing fully on everything he learned at Gruhn's and Guild. His flattop designs are drawn from the classic prewar Martins as well as '30s, '40s, and '50s Gibsons. His archtops are influenced by D'Angelicos, D'Aquistos, and Loars. The blue archtop guitar he built for collector Scott Chinery was displayed in 1998 at the Smithsonian Institute in Washington, D.C.

First year of production: 1974

Approximate annual production: 25

Percent custom instruments: 100

Types of guitars built: Steel-string flat-tops, archtops

Primary output: Steel-string flattops

Custom options: Trim, size, inlay, neck specs

Guitar pictured: p. 11

Walker Guitars
314 Pendleton Hill Rd.
N. Stonington, CT 06359
Phone: (860) 599-8753
www.walkerguitars.com

WEBBER GUITARS

David Webber has been working as a guitar builder since 1990 and has built nearly 500 acoustic instruments for customers worldwide. By combining hand craftsmanship with the precision and repeatability of computer-controlled machinery, he is able to build more than 100 instruments per year with one assistant. Vital tasks such as brace carving, neck fitting, and inlaying abalone are performed entirely by hand. Routine tasks like neck carving and roughing out bridges are efficiently performed by a computer-controlled router. This combination of old and new technologies allows Webber to build guitars that are precise, consistent, reliable, and affordable. His instruments are constructed in a humidity-controlled environment, which makes them stable and crack-resistant. His instruments are sold through a network of dealers throughout North America. They tend to be modern versions of traditional shapes, braced and built with his own techniques and patterns. He relies on the natural beauty of the woods rather than using excessive ornamentation and employs natural materials whenever possible.

First year of production: 1988

Approximate annual production: 100

Percent custom instruments: 70

Types of guitars built: Steel-string flat-tops, 12-strings, nylon-strings

Primary output: Steel-string flattops

Custom options: Woods, neck and bridge widths, decorative details

Guitar pictured: p. 49

Webber Guitars
1385 A Crown St.
North Vancouver, BC V7J 1G4
Canada
Phone: (604) 980-0315
www.webberguitars.com

WECHTER GUITARS

Abraham Wechter began his guitar-building career in the early '70s, making dulcimers and repairing guitars in Seattle, Washington. He apprenticed with Richard Schneider and was captivated by Schneider's art as well as the scientific work he was doing with Dr. Michael Kasha. Wechter worked with Schneider to develop prototypes for what later became the Mark project for Gibson Guitars and went on to become an independent consultant for Gibson. In 1984, when Gibson moved to Nashville, Wechter opted to remain in Michigan, where he set up his own shop and began to design and build his own guitars. Between 1985 and 1995 Wechter designed and built guitars for such well-known artists as John McLaughlin, Steve Howe, Al Di Meola, Giovanni, John Denver, Earl Klugh, and Jonas Hellborg. He currently builds custom steel-strings in his Paw Paw, Michigan, workshop.

First year of production: 1984
Approximate annual production: 600
Percent custom instruments: 15
Types of guitars built: Steel-string flattops, 12-strings, nylon-strings
Primary output: Steel-string flattops
Guitar pictured: p. 13

Wechter Guitars
PO Box 91
Paw Paw, MI 49079-0091
Phone: (616) 657-3479
Fax: (616) 657-5608
www.wechterguitars.com

MARK WESCOTT GUITARS

Mark Wescott's approach to guitar building is one of innovative design based on the importance of sound and the interaction between the guitar and the player. He built his first guitar in 1980 under the guidance of George Morris while attending the Charles Fox Guitar Research and Design Seminar. He continued his studies for three years as resident luthier at Richard Schneider's Lost Mountain Center for the Guitar. There he acquired a solid background in the Kasha method of radial soundboard bracing. The modified Kasha bracing and offset soundhole are the foundation of Wescott's work. The Kasha design is used for more controlled distribution of sound vibrations. Wescott's offset soundhole allows the instrument to be miked without interference from the player's hands. An additional advantage of his unusual soundhole placement is that it allows the best possible vibrating surface—the middle of the guitar—to resonate without interruption. Wescott has also continued to develop his guitars over the years through improvements in structural design.

First year of production: 1980
Approximate annual production: 5–6
Percent custom instruments: 100
Types of guitars built: Steel-string flattops
Custom options: Woods, neck dimensions, electronics

Mark Wescott Guitars
3 East Maple Shade Ln.
Marmora, NJ 08223
Phone: (609) 390-7710

WORLAND GUITARS

When Jim Worland built his first guitar in 1992, he was amazed by how much a custom instrument could improve the sound of his playing. Since then he has combined his career in design engineering with a love of art and music and founded Worland Guitars. In his workshop in Rockford, Illinois, he builds fine handcrafted instruments on a custom basis for players of all levels. Worland's instruments are designed and built to function first and foremost as tools for musicians. He specializes in small-bodied guitars, especially hybrid steel-string classicals for crossover players.

First year of production: 1997
Approximate annual production: 10
Percent custom instruments: 100
Types of guitars built: Steel-string flattops, 12-strings
Custom options: Vintage appointments, seven strings, classical-style necks
Guitar pictured: p. 38

Worland Guitars
810 N. First St.
Rockford, IL 61107
Phone: (815) 961-8854
www.worlandguitars.com

WRIGHT GUITAR TECHNOLOGY

Wright Guitar Technology was formed by luthier Rossco Wright, who had a 25-year career as a guitar repair technician. After seeing so many crunched, smashed guitars, he longed to build something that people could take with them so they could leave their beautiful, precious guitars safely at home. He dreamed of a product that maintained the essence of the joy of playing guitar but was affordable and unbreakable. He decided that the breakable peghead and the crunchable top, back, and sides had to go. Repair client and manufacturing consultant Frank Nakatsuma helped Wright get the product off the ground with technical and sales assistance. The product attracted the attention of CNN. This broadcast brought the attention of NASA, which took the guitar on the Space Shuttle Atlantis. It was given as a gift to a cosmonaut on board the Mir space station and orbited the Earth 12,160 times in two years. Wright and his five employees now manufacture the travel guitars in a little shop in Eugene, Oregon, where it rains a lot and life is good.

First year of production: 1993
Approximate annual production: 500
Percent custom instruments: 0
Types of guitars built: Steel-string flattops, nylon-strings
Primary output: Travel guitars

Wright Guitar Technology
4686B Isabelle

Eugene, OR 97402
Phone/fax: (541) 343-0872
www.soloette.com

YANUZIELLO STRINGED INSTRUMENTS

Joseph Yanuziello produces unique handcrafted acoustic and electric stringed instruments, everything from round- and square-neck resophonics to acoustic hollow-neck Hawaiians to octave mandolins. His 25-plus years of experience enable him to design and handcraft many of the hardware components on his instruments, such as the innovative and efficient bridge/tailpiece common to all Yanuziello electric instruments. He strives for a tone that acknowledges the roots of the instrument as well as excellent playability.

First year of production: 1980
Approximate annual production: 10–14
Percent custom instruments: 50
Types of guitars built: Resonator guitars, Hawaiian guitars, specialty guitars
Primary output: Resophonics and Hawaiians
Custom options: Scale length, neck and fingerboard dimensions, woods, inlays
Guitars pictured: pp. 89, 96

Yanuziello Stringed Instruments
442 Dufferin St., Studio H
Toronto, ON M6K 2A3
Canada
Phone: (416) 535-6018
Fax: (416) 535-1858
www.interlog.com/~ysi

J.R. ZEIDLER GUITARS

John Zeidler's career in lutherie began with the creation of a dulcimer at the age of 15. His first guitar, a 45-style dreadnought, was built in 1976 when he was 17. After a brief apprenticeship with Augustino LoPrinzi, Zeidler set up shop in Philadelphia. His line of instruments is representative of nearly 25 years of experimentation in design and construction of his own instruments as well as years of repair and restoration work on modern and vintage instruments. All Zeidler instruments feature hand-carved hardware (except for tuners) and inlays, and all his carved models are tap-tuned. Other features, such as his signature binding on the back of the peghead and handmade, violin-style finishes, are standard.

First year of production: 1977
Approximate annual production: 12
Percent custom instruments: 100
Types of guitars built: Steel-string flattops, 12-strings, archtops
Primary output: Archtops
Custom options: Woods, neck sizes, pickguards, electronics, engraved hardware, inlays
Guitars pictured: pp. 77, 83

J.R. Zeidler Guitars
1441 S. Broad St.
Philadelphia, PA 19147
Phone: (215) 271-6858
Fax: (215) 463-9085
www.zeidler.com

ZEILER GUITARS

Jamon Zeiler spent many years working as a singer-songwriter and a professional cabinetmaker before embarking on his lutherie career. He hears, feels, and senses what the wood and the craftsperson can ultimately bring to the player. Zeiler strives to make each of his guitars as unique as the person for whom it is created. He is committed to questioning, comparing, and challenging ordinary or accepted work. He has extensive repair and restoration experience with acoustic, electric, and classical guitars as well as violins, mandolins, and banjos. Doing repairs allows him to study a wide variety of instruments and designs.

First year of production: 1992
Approximate annual production: 8–9
Percent custom instruments: 100
Types of guitars built: Steel-string flattops, 12-strings, nylon-strings
Primary output: Steel-string flattops
Custom options: Everything is negotiable
Guitar pictured: p. 44

Zeiler Guitars
10767 Valiant Dr.
Cincinnati, OH 45231
Phone: (513) 607-0042
Fax: (513) 829-8341

GARY ZIMNICKI

Gary Zimnicki has built more than 125 guitars since he began building custom-made guitars in the '70s. He encourages his customers to get involved in the planning and design of their instruments. The result of these maker-player collaborations is a finely made guitar with exceptional tone, playability, and beauty. Each unique instrument is perfectly matched to the player's needs and desires. Most of Zimnicki's work is with archtop, flat-top steel-string, and classical guitars, and he has built a few classical guitars in the Schneider/Kasha style as well as a few mandolin-family instruments and several solid-body guitars and 12-strings.

First year of production: 1980
Approximate annual production: 15–20
Percent custom instruments: 100
Types of guitars built: Steel-string flattops, 12-strings, nylon-strings, archtops, specialty guitars
Guitar pictured: p. 62

Gary Zimnicki
15106 Garfield Ave.
Allen Park, MI 48101
Phone: (313) 381-2817
www.zimnicki.com

About the Authors

Julie Bergman is an L.A.-based writer, guitarist, photographer, and private investigator. She began playing folk and blues guitar at age 14 while living in the Boston area, performed locally, and traveled to the U.K. with an acoustic trio in the early 1970s. She booked musicians at Reflections, a Cambridge, Massachusetts, coffeehouse before moving to Los Angeles to work as a music publicist, tour assistant, and film studio administrator. She has experienced the joy of purchasing her own custom guitars, working closely with luthiers Kevin Ryan and Lance McCollum to hone in on two of her dream guitars.

Dana Bourgeois has enjoyed a notable career as a custom builder, repairer, designer, and manufacturer of acoustic guitars. Over the years his knowledge of guitar making has been widely circulated through various writing, lecturing, teaching, and consulting activities. Formerly associated with Martin, Schoenberg, Gibson, Paul Reed Smith, and Dana Bourgeois Guitars, Bourgeois currently builds custom handmade guitars in his shop in Lewiston, Maine.

William R. Cumpiano was born in Puerto Rico in 1945 and has been making guitars in the American, European, and Latin American traditions for more than 30 years. He builds his guitars by hand, one and two at a time, in his Northampton, Massachusetts, studio. He also teaches his craft and writes about his field in books, magazines, and on the Web at www.cumpiano.com. He is coauthor of the premier textbook in the field, *Guitarmaking: Tradition and Technology*, and is currently working on a new textbook about the myriad stringed instrument traditions of the U.S., Caribbean, and Central and South America.

Alex de Grassi was a pivotal player in the development of the solo fingerstyle guitar movement that began with Windham Hill Records in the late '70s. His 1978 recording *Turning, Turning Back* was a revelation to listeners and helped redefine the way we play and hear acoustic steel-string guitars. De Grassi has turned to custom guitar makers to meet his unique musical needs over the years and plays instruments built by George Lowden, Jeff Traugott, and Fred Carlson, among others. His most recent recording is a collection of jazz standards entitled *Bolivian Blues Bar* (Narada Jazz).

Ben Elder started taking guitar lessons in his hometown of Oklahoma City when he was 12. Thirty-four years later, he works for CBS television and the Blue Ridge Pickin' Parlor Music Store in the Los Angeles area and hosts a weekly bluegrass and old-time country radio show on KPFK called *Wildwood Flower*. Elder's collection of guitars reflects his obsession with Weissenborn-made instruments, and he is working on a book about Weissenborns and related hollow-neck Hawaiian guitars.

Teja Gerken managed a music store; apprenticed with a guitar maker in Paracho, Mexico; and worked as a freelance translator and desktop publisher before he became *Acoustic Guitar* magazine's gear editor. When he is not busy reviewing music equipment, Gerken hosts a fingerstyle concert series at an Emeryville, California, venue called Strings, where he has shared the stage with many of today's top pickers. His Web site, www.tejagerken.com, features articles on a variety of guitar-related subjects as well as samples of his debut CD *On My Way* (LifeRhythm Music).

Richard Johnston is a luthier, stringed-instrument repairman, and co-owner of Gryphon Stringed Instruments in Palo Alto, California. He is also co-author, with Jim Washburn, of the book *Martin Guitars: An Illustrated Celebration of America's Premier Guitarmaker* (Rodale Press). Johnston has been writing for *Acoustic Guitar* magazine since its inception in 1990 and has been a contributing editor since 1995. He has written definitive, historical articles on a wide variety of guitars, including vintage flattops, archtops, dreadnoughts, 12-frets, and the Gibson J-200.

Rick Turner has been designing, building, and repairing acoustic and electric guitars for 35 years. He cofounded the Alembic Corp. in the '70s, worked for the Gibson Guitar Corp., and later started his own cutting-edge company, Turner Guitars. He also designed magnetic pickups and cofounded Highlander Musical Audio Products. Turner is currently president of the Renaissance Guitar Corp. and recently completed an acoustic guitar for Henry Kaiser that is slated to travel to the South Pole. He is also a regular contributor to *Acoustic Guitar* magazine and has been a contributing editor since 1991.